Joy and Human Flourishing

Joy and Human Flourishing

Essays on Theology, Culture, and the Good Life

Miroslav Volf and Justin E. Crisp, editors

Fortress Press
Minneapolis

JOY AND HUMAN FLOURISHING

Essays on Theology, Culture, and the Good Life

Cover image: iStock/Thinkstock

Cover design: Ivy Palmer Skrade

Library of Congress Cataloging-in-Publication Data

Print ISBN: 978-1-4514-8207-2

eBook ISBN: 978-1-5064-0286-4

The paper used in this publication meets the minimum requirements of American National Standard for Information Sciences — Permanence of Paper for Printed Library Materials, ANSI Z329.48-1984.

Manufactured in the U.S.A.

This book was produced using Pressbooks.com, and PDF rendering was done by PrinceXML.

Contents

Introduction: A Bright Sorrow

Justin E. Crisp

> *The knowledge of the fallen world does not kill joy,*
> *which emanates in this world always, constantly, as a bright sorrow.*
> Alexander Schmemann

Why joy—and why now? It is perhaps counterintuitive for joy to occupy a central place in a Christian theology, or at least in a theology capable of taking seriously the state of the world in which we live. Have not the masters of suspicion sufficiently warned theologians away from commending religious sentiments that, in their spiritual purity, distract their subjects from the material situation of life and issue in a total flight from the world? Did not the manifold tragedies of the mid-twentieth century disabuse theologians once and for all of their Pollyanna-ish penchant for progress, their sure confidence in the sacred endowment of the ingenuity of human beings and their potential to build kingdoms of God on earth? Is not the perspective of Walter Benjamin's angel of history—that history is no "chain of events," and certainly not one moving toward a paradise, but "one single catastrophe which keeps piling wreckage upon wreckage and hurls it in front of his feet"[1]—the only credible theological perspective on life this side of the eschaton?

When we stand in the shadow cast by the towering wreckage of history, joy fails to stand out as the most obviously promising candidate among possible pivots of theological thinking. On the one hand, joy, an emotion, might seem too fickle or fragile to withstand the assault of suffering and the crushing magnitude of pain. Joy, taken in this instance to be tantamount to high-octane happiness, fades under duress and is incapable of being sustained by or sustaining someone across the vicissitudes of life. On the other hand, an injunction to be joyful might seem ethically irresponsible and politically dangerous, too close to peddling just one more religious opiate to the oppressed masses. To enjoin human beings to "rejoice always (!)," as does St. Paul (Phil. 4:4), might verge on a demand to be content with the status quo, to insist that one should be happy with whatever little one has and with any suffering that comes one's way and, thus, never question what material and social conditions have conspired to put one in one's place. As opiates do, such joy might, for a moment, minimally increase the quality of one's life, but it would do so to the detriment of the *dis*-content arguably necessary to motivate movements for substantial change.

The essays in this volume on joy and human flourishing wrestle with these concerns, among others. At their center is the conviction that joy stands at the very core of Christian faith, life, and practice, and that the dearth of sustained scholarly reflection on joy has left theologians bereft of a key resource for articulating a compelling vision of the good life capable both of pushing against the tide of suffering and of resisting the shifting tides of a culture unmoored from transcendence.[2]

1. Walter Benjamin, "Theses on the Philosophy of History," in *Illuminations*, ed. Hannah Arendt, trans. Harry Zohn (New York: Schocken Books, 2007), 257.

Whether by reason of the prevailing sentiment described above or some other motive, focused reflection on joy is strikingly absent from contemporary scholarly theology. Notable exceptions to this, of course, include Jürgen Moltmann's *Theology and Joy* (1973), Karl Barth's deeply eschatological account of joy in volume 3 of the *Church Dogmatics*, and Hans Urs von Balthasar's brief reflections on the relationship between joy and suffering in the Trinity in volume 5 of *Theo-Drama*.[3] These studies are, however, exceptions that largely prove the rule,[4] which stands in amazing contrast to the seeming ubiquity of joy in the Jewish and Christian Scriptures. The potential for theologians to mine the scriptural witnesses for these references is immense. In terms of a Christology, the life of Jesus is flanked at either end, as it were, by joy: the tidings of his birth ground a joy intended for all the world (Luke 2:10), and the saving interventions of

2. On the importance of the relation to transcendence and an account of the vital role religions stand to play in the public square insofar as they cast visions of the good life trading on the same, see Miroslav Volf, *Flourishing: Why We Need Religion in a Globalized World* (New Haven: Yale University Press, forthcoming 2016).

3. Jürgen Moltmann, *Theology and Joy* (London: SCM, 1973). Karl Barth, *Church Dogmatics*, vol. III/4, *The Doctrine of Creation* (Edinburgh: T&T Clark, 1956–75), 374–85. Hans Urs von Balthasar, *Theo-Drama: Theological Dramatic Theory*, vol. 5, *The Last Act*, trans. Graham Harrison (San Francisco: Ignatius, 1998), 250–56, 268.

4. The argument here is not simply that references to joy are rare in theological literature (such a thesis would be difficult to substantiate, in any case, even if it has incidentally proven true in our research), but that the disciplines of the modern theological academy have neglected to pursue studies giving joy the pride of place it, arguably, enjoys in the Scriptures. Noteworthy, too, is a promising increase in interest in joy, evidenced, for example, by the recent work of Ellen Charry (who echoes our sense of the lack of sustained reflection on joy in theological discourse and contributes to the diagnostics of why this is the case); see her *God and the Art of Happiness* (Grand Rapids: Eerdmans, 2010) and "The Necessity of Divine Happiness: A Response from Systematic Theology," in *The Bible and the Pursuit of Happiness: What the Old and the New Testaments Teach Us About the Good Life*, ed. Brent A. Strawn (New York: Oxford University Press, 2012). Joy serves, moreover, as the point of departure for Pope Francis's *The Joy of the Gospel: Apostolic Exhortation Evangelii Gaudium of the Holy Father Francis to the Bishops, Clergy, Consecrated Persons and the Lay Faithful on the Proclamation of the Gospel in Today's World*, 2013. See also the dissertations of John Mark Capper ("Karl Barth's Theology of Joy," PhD diss., University of Cambridge, 1998) and Đorđe Petrović (PhD diss., Pontificium Institutum Orientale, 2015). In getting the lay of the theological landscape with regard to joy, I am much indebted to the extensive research pursued by Mark Berner under the auspices of the John Templeton Foundation's Office of Strategic Initiatives.

his life hurtle toward joy as their telos (Heb. 12:2). In terms of a moral anthropology, joy is listed by St. Paul among the fruits of the Spirit (Gal. 5:22–23), and to "rejoice always" is, again, famously among the injunctions he issues to the church at Philippi (Phil. 4:4). In terms of the doctrine of God, the three parables of Luke 15—the parables of the lost sheep, the lost coin, and the prodigal son—all describe God's reaction to the repentance of sinners in terms of joy. This is an echo and amplification of the significance of joy in the Hebrew Bible, perhaps most clearly stated when Psalm 16 boldly declares that "in [God's] presence there is fullness of joy" (16:11).

These are but three examples of doctrines into which the biblical testimony on joy promises to breathe new life, and the essays in this volume treat many more. Together, they attempt to remedy the paucity of contemporary theological reflection on joy, to sketch in an admittedly provisional way its nature, and to map its potential ramifications for the whole of Christian life and doctrine, in the hope of occasioning a broader consideration of joy both within Christian discourse and outside it, among the members of what, we hope, will become an inter- (and non-) religious alliance for joy.

***

Though each of the essays stands on its own as a substantive contribution to the study of joy and to the discipline from which it hails—and biblical studies, systematic theology, pastoral theology, political theology, and ethics are all variously represented here—the volume as a whole moves in the following way.

We begin with an essay by Jürgen Moltmann that, rooted in reflection on his previous efforts toward a theology of joy, attempts to conceive of the whole of Christian faith, worship, and life in its terms. For him, "Christianity is a unique religion of joy," expressed in its liturgical feasts, its depiction of God, and its treatment of theodicy.[5] Motivating the whole of Moltmann's investigation here is a concern for how theologians can commend rejoicing when so many live under conditions of extreme suffering. The thick account of joy that follows points up the way in which human joy is grounded in God's own joy, famously depicted in the parables of Luke 15 as the abundant, excessive rejoicing of the father at the repentant return of the prodigal. Christian joy stands in contrast both to what Moltmann provocatively terms the "fun society" (*Spaßgesellschaft*) and to the opiate-like joy characteristic of Friedrich Schiller's "Ode to Joy." Instead, Christian joy both motivates dissatisfaction with conditions of suffering and is a deep wellspring of abiding hope in God's work of redemption: "Joy in life's happiness motivates us to revolt against the life that is destroyed and against those who destroy life. And grief over life that is destroyed is nothing other than an ardent longing for life's liberation to happiness and joy."[6] Moltmann's sketch of Christianity as a religion of joy introduces many of the key themes, scriptural passages, and sociopolitical questions treated in the other chapters of the volume and, thus, serves in large part as the frame for all that follows.

Next are two essays by Marianne Meye Thompson and N. T. Wright that treat the most important references to joy in the Jewish and Christian Scriptures. Thompson focuses on the Greek *chara* and identifies three strands of biblical thought on joy: joy as a good response to good things, joy over the removal of affliction and distress, and joy in the midst of affliction and distress. The first two constitute what Thompson denotes *joy because* (of something good), while the third constitutes *joy notwithstanding* (some deficiency). Nonetheless, *joy notwithstanding* is still rooted in *joy because* on

---

5. See Chapter 1, 6.
6. Ibid., 14.

account of its being made possible by the eschatological horizon of Christian discipleship. It consists in a *joy because* of God, in terms both of the consolation one enjoys by virtue of God's continuing presence in the midst of one's suffering and the hope one has in God's eschatological redemption of the evils one presently suffers.

For his part, Wright emphasizes the way in which biblical joy consists in "the fresh *presence* of God . . . [and] the fresh *act* of God," as God acts to save in accordance with God's promises.[7] He draws a helpful comparison between the balance of joy and hope in the worldviews of early Christianity and Second-Temple Judaism, suggesting that, on the whole, the former put the weight primarily on joy and the latter on hope. The reason for this, he speculates, is on account of the Christian conviction of the already-realized cosmic sovereignty of Jesus, exemplified particularly in Paul's letter to the Philippians. The Christian can "rejoice always" on account of Christ's already-binding lordship and is, indeed, enjoined to this end in order to bear public witness to his sovereignty, over and against the lordship of Caesar. Together, Thompson's and Wright's essays catalogue and map the bulk of biblical perspectives on joy, and they point us not to an otherworldly, passing sentiment but to the sturdy confidence in the good of the salvific working of God that is the wellspring of true rejoicing.

Following this is a detailed and programmatic sketch by Charles Mathewes of how the main loci of Christian theological reflection can be thrown open by organizing them around joy. Structuring Mathewes's theology of joy is an Augustinian anthropology of desire that posits partaking "in the endless joyful round of love that is the Trinity" as our end and eschatological destiny.[8] Joy itself consolidates the fundamental dynamics of Christian life, involving an agency

7. See Chapter 3, 48–49.
8. See Chapter 4, 65.

which Mathewes very helpfully describes in terms of "the middle voice": joy is genuinely our own response, and yet, it also comes to us as a gift—it is something that happens *to* us, and yet, also something in which we actively participate.[9] Mathewes proceeds to develop a robust ecclesiology of joy, conceiving of the churches as the sites in which God makes us "fit to bear the joy that is our eschatological destiny."[10] That is, the purpose of the churches is to be training grounds of right rejoicing, and the formation of persons undertaken in them has immediate and far-reaching political ramifications, fostering resistance particularly against the anesthetizing effects of joyless consumer capitalist culture (the diagnosis of which by Mathewes hearkens back to Moltmann's discussion of *Spaßgesellschaft*). Mathewes's theology of joy is a political theology insofar as it is a church theology, and a church theology insofar as it is a political theology.

Mary Clark Moschella, then, offers up a vision of how practices of pastoral care can be oriented around joy and its cultivation. Noting the dominance heretofore of a pathology-driven diagnostics imported into pastoral theology largely from Freudian psychoanalysis, Moschella strives to locate best practices of care that take the experience of joy as their telos and their source. Understanding joy as being rooted in one's giving attention to the goodness of God, she avers that joy shifts the human perspective from a logic of scarcity to one of abundance, making possible transformative visions of the world as it *could* (and should) be. On this accounting, pastoral theology and practice should take as its point of departure a holistic vision of flourishing, joyful life, rather than simply reacting to the manifold crises of human living as they come. Examples of practitioners of care of this sort abound for Moschella,

9. Ibid., 66–67.
10. Ibid., 65.

but for the purposes of the essay in question she takes as her primary test case the work of Paul Farmer, the founder of Partners in Health, whose life indicates two of the "seeds of joy" she thinks to be most integral to pastoral ministry: "a sense of vocation and a practice of compassion." She remarks that Farmer's joy offers him "access to a deep sense of hope, even in circumstances that are often daunting and sometimes painfully discouraging" and fuels his efforts to increase the well-being of the poor.[11] Pastoral theology stands to gain much from paying attention to the wellsprings of joy exemplified in the lives of Farmer and others, and Moschella's reflections very helpfully point the way forward for reconceiving pastoral practice primarily in terms of well-being rather than restricting its considerations to pathology-driven models of caregiving.

The volume culminates with Miroslav Volf's summary vision of a theology of joy, gathering up many of the various strands of thought set out in the other essays into a synthetic account of joy and its relation to the good life. He conceives of joy as an emotion having a particular object—and, indeed, a particular object perceived as a *good*. Joy is, as he puts it, an "emotional attunement between the self and the world—usually a small portion of it—experienced as blessing."[12] Volf presupposes an integrative account of the good life having three dimensions: agential (the good life is the life that is *lived well*), circumstantial (the good life is the life that *goes well*), and affective (the good life is the life that *feels good*). Joy is a summation of the affective dimension of the good life and, at the same time, consolidates *all three dimensions*. As an emotion that perceives its object as a good, joy requires that one's life is marked by a good (so, the life that goes well and is led well) and that one is properly oriented to this good *as* good. Joy is, therefore, the *crown* of the good life, not simply in

11. See Chapter 5, 113, 118, 124.
12. See Chapter 6, 130.

that it is its third and final dimension—the proverbial icing on the cake, as it were—but more properly in that joy is the expression and manifestation of the good life, just as the crown is an expression and public manifestation of royal authority. On Volf's account, joy cannot be given adequate exposition without making reference to the good life, and, likewise, the good life cannot be envisioned in its fullness without reference to joy.

***

At this point, let us revisit the twin concerns raised at the outset regarding suffering and ideological alienation by teasing out, briefly, just two of the most common strands of thought among the essays assembled here.

First of all, suffering presents perhaps the most urgent challenge to a theology of joy. Wright and Thompson are pushed by Pauline passages like Romans 5–8 ("We also boast in our sufferings" [Rom. 5:3]) to posit *some* relationship between suffering and joy—even to such an extent that Wright himself avers that this is not "joy *despite* suffering, but . . . joy *because of* suffering."[13] Nonetheless, both Wright and Thompson understand the joy in suffering described by St. Paul as being made conceivable in terms of sharing in Christ's own suffering: as Thompson puts it, "In that sense, *joy notwithstanding* is indeed a joy *because of*, that is, joy because Paul is joined precisely *in* his suffering to the Lord Jesus Christ who 'will transform the body of our humiliation that it may be conformed to the body of his glory' (Phil. 3:21)."[14] Considered along these lines, it is not suffering per se that is the cause of Paul's declaration that "we also boast in our sufferings" but, rather, a sharing in the sufferings of *Christ*, on

13. See Chapter 3, 55.
14. See Chapter 2, 29-30.

account of which Paul hopes also to share in Christ's resurrection. As Thompson emphasizes, this means that one cannot properly rejoice *in* suffering or injustice but only rejoice *notwithstanding* suffering and injustice and in their midst. This principle is thrown into further relief by Volf, who explicitly describes taking suffering *itself* as the object of one's rejoicing as "masochistic"; rather, one is made able to rejoice rightly notwithstanding conditions of suffering on account "of some good that is ours despite the suffering (for instance, God's character, deeds, and the promise of redemption) or because of a good the suffering will produce (for instance, a child for a mother in childbirth)."[15] The surprising realization that experiences of joy are compossible with situations of suffering marks not just the resilience of joy in itself but the particular resilience of religious joy, whose object is God. Moltmann goes so far as to assert that the condition of possibility for both suffering and joy are the same—the opening up of oneself to the other in which *love* consists. "Compassion," he writes, "is the other side of the living joy."[16] We might, with good reason, call joy of this sort "a bright sorrow," following Alexander Schmemann.[17] As the bright sorrow of this present dispensation, *joy notwithstanding* implicates one in the economy of redemption, in the drama of God's turning of our mourning into dancing (Ps. 30:11). All of these constitute promising points of departure for future clarification of this precarious nexus.

Second, joy pursues an oblique politics. As Volf puts it, that joy would be political at all is "surprising, because joy doesn't explicitly advocate any values or social ideals." True joy does, however, involve a right relationship to the good in which one rejoices, and joy,

---

15. See Chapter 6, 131.
16. See Chapter 1, 14.
17. Alexander Schmemann, *The Journals of Father Alexander Schmemann 1973–1983*, trans. Juliana Schmemann (Crestwood, NY: St. Vladimir's Seminary Press, 2000), 137.

as an "eternity-seeking" emotion (Nietzsche), wills the perpetual continuation of that good. "In this willing," Volf avers, "joy sets itself tacitly against features of the world over which one cannot or should not rejoice, and does so without resentment or judgment."[18] This *joy against* the world[19] aligns well with Wright's suggestion that joy is the outward, public manifestation of Christian conviction in the lordship of Christ. Insofar as the joy of early Christians was rooted in the already-realized sovereignty of Christ, it set itself against the alternate sovereignty of Caesar. Joy issues glad tidings "of a different empire, a different *kind* of empire,"[20] one that fundamentally reconfigures our preconceived notions of sovereignty precisely by way of the manner in which it is brought about: crucifixion and resurrection. The capacity of joy to stand *against* the world is likewise echoed by Mathewes, who finds in an ecclesial "soul crafting and community creation" aimed toward cultivating dispositions of joy a profound resource for combating, for instance, the deadening fog of consumer culture. The political intervention here is, indeed, oblique on the churches' part, but its efficacy is secured on account of the fact that "the maladies of the soul that the churches diagnose are not unrelated to the maladies of the polity that much political discourse currently laments."[21] It is Moltmann who perhaps best encapsulates the politics of *joy against*—which, for him, always already raises the question of the relation between joy and suffering. Joy is, itself, the wellspring of motivation for revolt against injustice insofar as joy casts a positive vision of what life is truly *for*: "Otherwise we would accept innocent suffering and destroyed life as our fate and destiny,"[22] acquiescing

---

18. See Chapter 6, 132.
19. Willie Jennings has very provocatively (and helpfully) described this as "joy *contra mundi*" in a paper prepared for one of the Templeton Foundation-linked consultations on joy at the Yale Center for Faith and Culture. See his "Joy That Gathers," http://faith.yale.edu/sites/default/files/jennings_-_joy_that_gathers.pdf.
20. See Chapter 3, 61.
21. See Chapter 4, 69-70.

in resignation to the vision of history so powerfully depicted by Benjamin's angel.

On the accounting put forth in these essays, joy is neither an ideological opiate serving to placate and pacify the dispossessed, nor a sentiment as fragile as garden-variety happiness and, thus, as incapable of weathering situations of exigent suffering and stress. Joy, we think, stands to fund both perseverance and critique, both resilience and resistance. The bright sorrow of joy as we experience it in our present dispensation is but a foretaste of the abundant delight that will characterize the eschatological banqueting of the coming kingdom, the fullness of rejoicing that will consist in our sharing in the very joy of the triune God. These essays are offered in invitation to further reflection on joy and the concrete dispositions in which human flourishing consists, pursued with attention to the shadow cast by the towering wreckage of history and the resurrection splendor of glory radiating behind it.

22. See Chapter 1, 14.

Christianity: A Religion of Joy

Jürgen Moltmann

Once before I have written a theology of joy. This was in 1971 on the climax of the Vietnam War and the worldwide protest-movement against it. This was in the midst of student rebellions and the liberation movements in the third world. The German title was *Die ersten Freigelassenen der Schöpfung. Versuche über die Freude an der Freiheit und das Wohlgefallen am Spiel* ("The first liberated men in creation: experiments on the joy of freedom and the pleasure of play")—the English title was *Theology and Joy*.[1]

My question at that time was this: How can we laugh and rejoice, when there are so many tears to be wiped away and when new tears are being added every day? "How could we sing the Lord's song in a

---

1. Jürgen Moltmann, *Theology and Joy* (London: SCM, 1973); see also *Theology of Play* (New York: Harper & Row, 1972).

foreign land?" complains Psalm 137, as so many old spirituals echo.[2] How can one rejoice when innocent people are killed in Vietnam? How can one laugh and play when children are starving in Africa? How can we dance when in the prisons of Latin American military dictatorships human beings are tortured and "disappear"? Don't we live in *one* world? Do we have a right to joy if we do not cry out for those who suffer?

At that time the play *Anatevka*, or *Fiddler on the Roof*, made the circuit of our stages.[3] It tells of Tevye, the dairyman, and his Jewish congregation in the Ukranian village of Anatevka. The czar is oppressing them with excessive taxation. Their sons have to serve in a strange army and fight in unwanted wars. The Cossacks initiate pogroms against them whenever it strikes their fancy to go after the Jews. Still, this small congregation of the persecuted and pursued sings the Lord's song in an alien land. Are they doing this merely to forget their ugly predicament? Are they only trying to comfort themselves by covering their sadness with happy sounds? Or is there really such a thing as freedom in the midst of slavery, joy in the midst of suffering, and praise of God in the groaning of his creatures?

In this essay on God's joy and human flourishing I am not asking, "How can I sing the Lord's song in an alien land?" but, "How can I sing the Lord's song in his presence—figuratively speaking, in the warmth of God's shining face?" I am presupposing the contrasts of 1971, because from a global perspective, they are not diminishing, but now I want to explore the positive dimensions of the *great joy* in the *broad place* of God, who is nearer to us than we believe and is enlarging our life more than we think. Joy is the power to live, to love, to have creative initiative. Joy awakens all our senses, energizing mind and body. How do we experience this power in the presence

2. James H. Cone, *The Spirituals and the Blues: An Interpretation* (New York: Seabury, 1972).
3. Moltmann, *Theology and Joy*, 26–28.

of the "living God" (Pss. 42:2, 84:2)? How is our life resonating the immense joy of God?

The Joy of God

In the Old Testament it is God's turning towards his people and his shining countenance that provokes joy:

> You show me the path of life.
> In your presence there is fullness of joy;
> in your right hand are pleasures for evermore. (Ps. 16:11)

Blessings are proceeding from the shining countenance of God, and a blessed life is life in fullness and festivity. Human beings are not the only creatures who flourish in the presence of God, though, for it is also—and perhaps in the first place—the nature of the earth:

> Let the heavens be glad, and let the earth rejoice;
> let the sea roar, and all that fills it;
> let the field exult, and everything in it.
> Then shall all the trees of the forest sing for joy
> before the Lord; for he is coming,
> for he is coming to judge the earth.
> He will judge the world with righteousness,
> and the peoples with his truth. (Ps. 96:11–13)

When God comes to judge the earth, the whole of creation will rejoice. We should have this in mind when we speak of the final judgment. The final judgment is a day of rejoicing, not of terror.[4]

When God comes to human beings there are two turning movements. First in God: God turning from a "hidden face" (*hester panim*) to a "shining face." This conversion in God from God's

---

4. Jürgen Moltmann, *Sun of Righteousness, Arise! God's Future for Humanity and the Earth* (Minneapolis: Fortress Press, 2010), 127–48.

aversion to human sin to God's affection of grace evokes in human beings a corresponding turning movement:

> You have turned my mourning into dancing;
> you have taken off my sackcloth
> and clothed me with joy. (Ps. 30:11)

> Let me hear joy and gladness;
> let the bones that you have crushed rejoice. . . .
> Restore to me the joy of your salvation,
> and sustain in me a willing spirit. (Ps. 51:8, 12)

> And the ransomed of the Lord shall return, and come to Zion with singing; everlasting joy shall be upon their heads; they shall obtain joy and gladness, and sorrow and sighing shall flee away. (Isa. 35:10)

> God himself "will renew you in his love; he will exult over you with loud singing" (Zeph. 3:17).

With this composition from the Psalms and the prophets of Israel we see a great and wonderful harmony: the joyous and singing God, the joy of the earth, and the joy of the redeemed people.

The Birth of Religion out of the Feast of Life

According to modern theories of religion, religion is alive in the misfortune of the people: "Religion is the sigh of the oppressed creature" and an "opium" of suffering and desperate people, said Karl Marx.[5] Religion must be "necessary," because everything in the modern world must be necessary; otherwise it is superfluous and useless. As a common proverb says, "Need leads to prayer." But this view is wrong. In truth, religion is the feast of life, useless but joyful, and prayer is praise for the fortune of being.[6]

---

5. Karl Marx, "Contribution to the Critique of Hegel's *Philosophy of Right*," in *The Marx-Engels Reader*, ed. Robert C. Tucker, 2nd ed. (New York: W. W. Norton & Company, 1978), 54.

6. Theo Sundermeier, *Religion—was ist das? Religionswissenschaft im theologischen Kontext* (Frankfurt: O. Lembeck, 2007).

Primitive religions are *family religions*. They accompany life from birth to maturity, from weddings to anniversaries, and, at last, into the beyond. There are also festive celebrations of the natural circles of the earth, solstices, times of the moon, spring and autumn, seedtime and harvesting. These are the so-called *religions of nature*. Family religions and nature religions are the normal and everyday fundaments of all religions.

What happens in these feasts of life? It is the self-representation of living things and the "demonstrative value of their being." The biologists Adolf Portmann and Frederik Buytendijk have shown this in the world of animals: "To put it simply, the birds are singing much more than Darwin permits." In view of the extravagant luxury of specific types, of colorful splendor and hypertelic forms in the world of living things, Buytendjik contends with Portmann that nature's purpose-free abundance leads to this concept of self-representation.[7] This demonstrative value of being ascends through the stages of living things and reaches its completion in the human being's feast of life. Is not the free self-representation of human beings a human echo of God's pleasure in his creation? The glorification of God lies in any case in the festive demonstration of the human joy of existence. Human beings in their fondness for this finite life and by their affirmation of mortal beauty share in the infinite pleasure of the Creator of this world.

In the feast, life is not produced but demonstrated. In these demonstrations, life experiences are articulated. There can be no experience of life without its adequate expression. Only when we can express our sorrow and joy have we made these *experiences*. It is not necessary but very meaningful and liberating to express the joy of

---

7. Frederik Jacobus Johannes Buytendijk, *Het Spel van Mensch en Diet als openbaring van levensdriften* (Amsterdam, 1932); Adolf Portmann, *Biologie und Geist* (Freiburg: Herder, 1963), 22–29.

existence in praise, thanksgiving, singing, and dancing and to find the right bodily and sensuous forms. The feast of life gives wings to the soul and new energies to the body. It is renewing life out of the transcendent origin of life.

Christianity: The Religion of Joy

If we really think about it, we arrive at a surprising conclusion: Christianity is a unique religion of joy. Faith is living in the Christian feasts. And yet the universal symbol of Christianity is the cross, a symbol of pain, suffering, and cruel death. How do these things go together? Are joy and pain contradictions, or do they belong together?

Christianity begins with *Christmas*. When Mary becomes pregnant with Jesus, she sings,

> My soul magnifies the Lord,
> and my spirit rejoices in God my Savior. (Luke 1:46–47)

When her child is born in the stable in Bethlehem, angels visit the poor and freezing shepherds in the field:

> Do not be afraid; for see—I am bringing you good news of great joy for all the people: to you is born this day in the city of David a Savior, who is the Messiah, the Lord. (Luke 2:10–11)

According to the Eastern church, this birth of the divine child happened not in a man-made stable but in a cave of the earth: he is also the Savior of the earth! This birth is embraced by God's joy and received by the joy of human beings and the earth. This is why today we still sing cheerful Christmas hymns and carols and give each other gifts as ways to express our joy.

> Joy to the world! The Lord is come:
> Let earth receive her king.

Whereas Christmas is the central festival of Western Christianity, *Easter* is the central festival of *Eastern Christianity*. The resurrection of Christ from the dead and the appearance of eternal life in him are the inexhaustible grounds for Easter jubilation:

> Christ is risen—he is risen indeed!

In a canon of John Damascene for the feast of Easter we read,

> Rejoice ye heavens in worthy wise!
> Earth too shout for joy!
> Exult greatly, O cosmos,
> the visible and the invisible both.
> Christ was awoken. He the Joy of the aeons.[8]

In the West, too, we sing with Charles Wesley,

> Christ the Lord is risen today!
> Sons of men and angels say:
> Raise your joy and triumph high;
> Sing, ye heavens, and earth reply.

Both East and West know that the resurrection of Christ is not just a human event but a cosmic event as well. The Easter rejoicing embraces the whole groaning creation. Easter jubilation is also the joy of the earth as indicated in the Psalms of the Old Testament. Therefore we celebrate Easter in springtime, the European springtime, as a sign for the final spring of the new, eternal creation of all things.

Finally, at Whitsun or Pentecost, joyful hymns extol the experience of God's Spirit in the life of men and women. Pentecost is the central festival of the new *Pentecostal churches*. Whenever there is talk in the New Testament about experiences of the divine Spirit

---

8. Ernst Benz, *Heiteres Licht der Herrlichkeit: die Glaubenswelt der Ostkirche* (Hamburg: Furche, 1962), 2.

we hear words of joy. For it is the Spirit of life that fills human beings with a new and enduring feeling about life, an experience that opens soul and senses for the nearness of God.

> My heart and my flesh sing for joy to the living God. (Ps. 84:2)

These are not only "spiritual joys" but also the joys of senses. We don't have to differentiate between spiritual and sensual happiness. They belong together. But we must differentiate between the joys of life and destructive addictions, that which the New Testament calls "carnal sins," that is, sickness unto death.

And what about Good Friday, the central feast day of *Lutheran Christians*? Certainly here thoughts of compassion turn first of all to Christ's passion, his suffering with us and for us on the cross.

> O sacred head, now wounded,
> with grief and shame bowed down.

And yet, in another hymn:

> We sing the praise of him, who died,
> of him, who died upon the cross.

In the same hymn we call the cross of Christ "the balm of life, the cure of woe." *Ave crux—spes unica*. Behind the cross of Christ the sun of resurrection arises.

It is a remarkable fact that the great Christian festivals are not distributed throughout the year but take place in the first half and are concentrated on the spring. The spring of the new year begins with the winter solstice, comes alive at Easter in the flowers and trees, and reaches its full flowering at Whitsun or Pentecost. This is, in my understanding, a way of showing that with the coming of Christ into this world, his death and resurrection, and the outpouring of the divine Spirit, the spring of eternal life begins for human beings, all living beings, and the earth. Mortal and earthly life is taken up into the divine, eternal, and heavenly life.

The Joy of the Seeking and Finding God

In the fifteenth chapter of his Gospel, Luke interprets the astonishing—and, by the Pharisees, denounced—attitude of Jesus, "This fellow welcomes sinners and eats with them" (Luke 15:2), with three well-known parables: about the widow's lost and found coin, about the lost and found sheep, which the shepherd carries on his shoulders home, and about the lost son, whom his father folds in his arms.[9] Luke's theological interpretation of the found coin and the found sheep is the following:

> Just so, I tell you, there will be more joy in heaven over one sinner who repents than over ninety-nine righteous people who need no repentance. (Luke 15:7)

This theology is not quite correct, because first, Jesus accepted "sinners and tax collectors" without conditions and did not have table communion with only repenting sinners, and second, the lost sheep could do nothing to contribute to its being found, and the lost coin could not repent. The joy is only on the side of the finder. These are parables of God's love for the lost and of God's joy in finding them. Jesus had demonstrated this in accepting sinners without conditions and eating with them. Only the lost son is "repenting," turning around from the way toward perishing and coming home. Before he can confess his sins, however, his father, seeing from afar, runs toward him and enfolds him in his arms (Luke 15:20). Prevenient grace is the joy of the father:

---

9. Julius Schniewind, *Die Freude der Buße* (Göttingen: Vandenhoeck & Ruprecht, 1956).

9

"For this son of mine was dead and is alive again; he was lost, and is found!" And they began to celebrate. (Luke 15:24)

The activity lies solely in the hands of the seeking and finding and rejoicing God. Repentance means to join in the rejoicing of God. Repentance is not self-afflicted pain or self-punishment; repentance is the joy of God. God seems to take pleasure in finding the lost. It is the lost and forgotten people in whom this joy of God springs up, not the self-satisfied and complacent.

A good witness for this is the famous seventeenth-century French mathematician and philosopher Blaise Pascal. When he died in Paris, a writing was found sewn into his coat, his so-called *Memorial*:

> "God of Abraham, God of Isaac, God of Jacob," not of philosophers and scholars.
> Certainty, certainty, heartfelt, joy, peace.
> God of Jesus Christ. . . .
> Thy God shall be my God. . . .
> Joy, joy, joy, tears of joy.
> I have cut myself off from him. . . .
> My God wilt thou forsake me?
> Let me not be cut off from him for ever! . . .
> Jesus Christ.
> Jesus Christ.
> I have cut myself off from him, shunned him. . . .
> Let me never be cut off from him! . . .
> Everlasting joy in return for one day's effort on earth.[10]

Human Joy and Happiness

With this we change from a theology to an anthropology of joy, but we still keep God's joy in human beings and human joy in the living God before our eyes as the yardstick. If we do that, then joy cannot

---

10. Blaise Pascal, *Pensées sur la religion et sur quelques autres sujets*, ed. Louis Lafuma (Paris: Editions de Luxembourg, 1951), § 913. *Pensées*, trans. A. J. Krailsheimer (Baltimore: Penguin Books, 1966), 309–10.

be understood as a fleeting emotional state but only as a feature of a flourishing life, a life that is lived well and that goes well, as Miroslav Volf has put it.

Here the distinction between *joy* and *fun* is helpful. Today in the wealthier societies and the rising middle classes, we are living in a "fun society" (*Spaßgesellschaft*). I want to have a good time, say those young people who can afford it, and go to parties, preferring discos that are so noisy one can't hear oneself speak—but then, it isn't intended for one to speak and listen there. The sole idea is to be "beside oneself" in the dancing throng. Once one has had one's fun, one is not satisfied but is still hungry for more of it, pining for more, as if, in Shakespeare's words, the appetite had grown from what it fed upon. Life is expected to be a party without end. The older rich people have their cocktail parties, where they exchange courtesies and niceties or watch each other suspiciously. They no longer know how to celebrate a feast. They don't even try. They instead engage entertainers, event managers, and animateurs. They let themselves be entertained because they can't entertain themselves.

The difference between joy and fun is as great as the distinction between joy and a gamble of chance, or between a meaningful life and a lottery win. Joy is enduring and puts its mark on one's attitude to living. Fun is short-term and serves amusement. True joy is only possible with one's whole heart, whole soul, and all one's energies. The feeling about life that underlies the party-making fun society is, I suspect, more boredom with life than true joy. True joy opens the soul, is a flow of spirits, giving our existence a certain easiness. We may *have* fun, but we *are* in joy. In true joy, the ecstatic nature of human existence comes to expression.[11] We are created for joy. We are born for joy.

---

11. Helmuth Plessner, *Lachen und Weinen* (Bern: Francke, 1961), 93–100: the gestures of joy.

Joy and Human Pain

On the other hand, joy in life and happiness is denigrated when people incline to pain and sorrow rather than to joy and laughter. Do we have a right to happiness when so many people despair because their life is full of pain and sorrow? They think that grief is deeper than joy, that pain weighs more heavily than happiness, and that suffering seems more a matter of course than laughter. Their lives are more of tragedies than celebrations. After two world wars and unspeakable war crimes, Germans especially were more inclined to a tragic feeling for life, believing more in catastrophes than in successes and progress. In that terrible twentieth century, pessimism about the course of the world and a nihilistic view of human nature seemed more realistic than the idealism of the nineteenth century. I can illustrate this from Schiller's "Ode to Joy," which a few years ago was turned into the "Europe Hymn" in its setting in Beethoven's ninth symphony. After the world war terrors and so many state crimes, does Europe deserve this song of joy? Let's take a closer look:

Joy, thou beauteous godly lightning,
Daughter of Elysium,
Fire drunken we are ent'ring
Heavenly, thy holy home!
Thy enchantments bind together,
What did custom stern divide,
Every man becomes a brother,
Where thy gentle wings abide.

In the following verse we read,

Suffer on courageous millions!
Suffer for a better world!
O'er the tent of stars unfurl'd
God rewards you from the Heavens.[12]

The universal harmony is established with the help of the "next world," such that here on earth the "millions" of poor and oppressed people endure their suffering patiently and do not protest or revolt. Are these the costs of the ideal joy of humankind?

Schiller's "theodicy of joy" (George Steiner) soon evoked angry reactions on the part of protest atheists: the senseless sufferings of the "millions" cannot be compensated by a heavenly reward in the next world. Unjust suffering was the rock of atheism in the nineteenth century in Germany, and it was Dostoyevsky who took up arms against Schiller's joy idealism and countered his consolatory views with Ivan Karamazov's outraged story: While he was playing in the courtyard a little boy happened to injure the lord of the manor's favorite dog. As a punishment, the owner of the dog has the boy on the next morning torn to pieces by his hunting dogs, in front of his mother's eyes. Ivan's comment is as follows:

> And what becomes of *harmony*, if there is *hell*? . . . And if the sufferings of children go to swell the sum of sufferings which was necessary to pay for truth, then I protest that the truth is not worth such a price. . . . And so I hasten to give back my entrance ticket, and if I am an honest man I am bound to give it back as soon as possible. And that I am doing. It's not God that I don't accept, Alyosha, only I most respectfully return Him the ticket [to his world].[13]

Accordingly, I prefer to hold on to unrequited suffering and to protest against such injustice. This world, in which there are crimes and sufferings like this, is not a divine world of joy; it is hell. Nor is

---

12. Friedrich Schiller, "An die Freude/Ode to Joy," trans. by William F. Wertz, Schiller Institute, http://www.schillerinstitute.org/transl/schiller_poem/ode_to_joy.pdf. Schiller was influenced by the philosophy of Freemasonry just as was Mozart in his *Zauberflöte*.
13. Fyodor Dostoyevsky, *The Brothers Karamazov*, trans. Constance Garnett (New York: The Modern Library, 1929), 301; emphasis mine. On the relationship of Dostoyevsky to Schiller at this point, see George Steiner, *Tolstoy or Dostoevsky: An Essay in the Old Criticism*, 2nd ed. (New Haven: Yale University Press, 1996), 329, 331, 334.

there any imaginable compensation for this pain in a world beyond. The face of this world is not peace and joy. It is pain and protest.

But are joy and protest, happiness and pain, laughter and tears true alternatives? I don't believe they are. The secret of life is *love*. In love we go out of ourselves and lay ourselves open to all the experiences of life. In the love of life we become happy and vulnerable at the same time. In love we can be happy and sad. In love we can laugh and weep. In love we can rejoice and must protest at the same time. The more deeply love draws us into life, the more alive and, simultaneously, the more capable of sorrow we become. That is the dialectic of the affirmed and loved life. We can't have the first without the second. We can easily make the counterproof: when we are wounded and resigned and withdraw love from life, we lose interest in living and become apathetic. Then we no longer feel the disappointments, the injustice, and the pains, but we don't really live anymore either. We are spiritually petrified, and our hearts turn to stone. Nothing touches us either, neither good nor evil, and that is the first step on the road to death. It is the death of the soul, which goes ahead of the death of a person.

This means that Schiller's "Ode to Joy" and Dostoyevsky's indignation about the innocent suffering of a child are not in fact antitheses, and we don't have to choose between them. Joy in life's happiness motivates us to revolt against the life that is destroyed and against those who destroy life. And grief over life that is destroyed is nothing other than an ardent longing for life's liberation to happiness and joy. Otherwise we would accept innocent suffering and destroyed life as our fate and destiny. Compassion is the other side of the living joy. We don't accuse God because there is suffering in the world. Rather, we protest in the name of God against suffering and those who cause it.

Finally, we ask which is greater: the joy or the grief, the happiness or the pain, life or death? And my answer is this: existence is greater than nonexistence, life is more than death, hope is above despair, and so joy is greater than pain. Why? The answer is simple: because whereas in pain we want our suffering to disappear, in joy we want the things that make us so happy to endure. That is why "Zarathustra spoke," according to Friedrich Nietzsche:

Joy—deeper still than misery:
Pain says: Refrain!
Yet all joy wants eternity—
—Wants deep, wants deep eternity.[14]

Why then is Christianity such a unique religion of joy, even though at its center stands the suffering of God and the cross of Christ? Because we remember the death of Christ in the light of his resurrection, and we remember his resurrection in the splendor of the divine, eternal life that is embracing our human and mortal life already here and now. This is the logic of "how much more" (Paul Ricoeur): where sin is powerful, God's grace is much more powerful (Rom. 5:20), for Christ has died, but how much more is Christ risen and has he overcome death (Rom. 8:38–39)! So pain too will be caught up and gathered into joy, despair into hope, and temporal death into the joy of divine life. Pains are passing, and I hear praise everlasting.

14. Friedrich Nietzsche, *Thus Spoke Zarathustra*, ed. Adrian Del Caro and Robert B. Pippin, trans. Adrian Del Caro (New York: Cambridge University Press, 2006), 264.

2

———

Reflections on Joy in the Bible

Marianne Meye Thompson

In studying the topic of joy in the Scriptures, several methodological challenges immediately present themselves. Perhaps the most pressing of them concerns the proper entry point for such a study. The most direct way into the topic would seem to be through a word or words for "joy." But which word or words? Should the net be cast broadly to include any and all passages in which one finds the ideas of joy, gladness, blessedness, celebration, and the like, or somewhat more narrowly, focusing perhaps on passages that include particular words?[1] Should we identify key words in the Hebrew or

---

1. Joy and happiness are sometimes distinguished, typically by noting that while the Bible promises joy, it does not promise (the more fleeting) happiness. The NRSV uses "happiness" once in its translation (Lam. 3:17), where the Hebrew has *ṭôbâ*, "good things, goodness, happiness" as does the LXX (*agatha*, "good things"). But see now the collection of essays, *The Bible and the Pursuit of Happiness: What the Old and New Testaments Teach Us about the Good Life*, ed.

17

Greek through which to investigate our subject or begin with the English translations and work backward?[2] Do we start with an idea of what joy is and include all passages that seem to flesh out our prior understanding, whether or not words related to "joy" actually appear in them?

In this chapter we will use the Greek word *chara* ("joy") and cognates as the lens through which to focus our work.[3] There are good reasons for such a choice. The word is important in the New Testament. Luke uses it in speaking of the "great joy" that comes through the gift of salvation in Christ (*charan megalēn*; Luke 2:10; cf. 24:52; Acts 15:3). In the farewell discourse of John, Jesus speaks frequently of the full or perfect joy that he will give the disciples (15:11; 16:20–24; 17:13). Paul uses the term often, and he includes joy in a definition of the kingdom of God (Rom. 14:17) and in his

Brent A. Strawn (Oxford: Oxford University Press, 2012). The appendix, "A Biblical Lexicon of Happiness" (323–70), a far-ranging compilation of terms related to "happiness" and "the good life," includes words such as "encourage" (*parakaleō*), "love, like, kiss" (*phileō*), "eat one's fill" (*chortazō*), and "satisfy" (*empiplēmi*). The essays related to the NT (on the Beatitudes, Luke–Acts, Paul, and apocalyptic literature) include particular discussion of passages that speak of being "blessed" or "happy" (*makarios*). Hence, the coverage and approach are somewhat different from that taken here.

2. The difficulties in limiting or selecting passages for examination can be illustrated by Psalm 126:2, which in the NRSV reads, "Our mouth was filled with *laughter*" (MT *śĕḥóq*), but in the LXX (125:2), "Our mouth was filled with *joy*" (*eplēsthē charas to stoma hēmōn*). We might not consider "joy" a good translation for "laughter," but the translator of the LXX apparently saw some appropriate nuance here; the earliest Christians who read their Bible in Greek would have read "joy" at this point. Presumably "laughter" and "joy" might be related; but we would not collapse the two, and we could surely distinguish the causes of laughter from the causes of joy.

3. In his book *Joy in the New Testament* (Grand Rapids: Eerdmans, 1984), William Morrice discusses the following word groups in the NT: *agallian, euthymein, euphrainein, hēdonē, tharsein, hilaros, kauchasthai, makarios, skirtan, chairein, synchairein*. Morrice assigns to each a nuance of meaning (exultant joy, optimism, good cheer, pleasure, courage, hilarity, and the like). His study underscores, rather than addresses or resolves, the methodological question we are raising here: What should count as evidence to understand "joy"? Apparently because Morrice's subject is joy in the New Testament, he investigates other Greek literature, including the LXX, but does not take the Hebrew into account. In this study, I have not considered words or ideas such as *hēdonē* ("pleasure"), *tharsein* ("to be courageous"), *kauchasthai* ("to boast"), or some of the others in Morrice's list, nor have I considered many of the terms in the "lexicon" in *The Bible and the Pursuit of Happiness*.

list of the fruits of the Spirit (Gal. 5:22). Indeed, the word and its cognates appear several dozen times throughout the New Testament. But, curiously, "joy" (*chara*) seldom occurs in the Psalms or prophets or, for that matter, in the Septuagint as a whole. Perhaps the book of Isaiah provides the most interesting data on that score. As is well known, Isaiah speaks frequently of the rejoicing that accompanies the coming age of salvation. But in the Septuagint of Isaiah the word *chara* itself is rare (e.g. Isa. 39:2, LXX only; 55:12; 66:10). The more frequent, often paired, words translated "joy and gladness" typically render the Greek *euphrosynēn kai agalliama* (e.g., Isa. 51:3).[4]

In this chapter I identify three patterns or clusters of texts in the Bible that relate to human expressions of gladness, rejoicing, and joy. Taken together, these patterns help us to sketch the biblical witness to what we call "joy." The first cluster of biblical texts describes human response to a variety of occasions or events, such as friendship or a wedding or tasting good food, in terms of joy, gladness, singing or shouting for joy, or rejoicing. There is a good way that human beings respond to the good things of life; in turn, these various things are known as good because they elicit this response of rejoicing.

In a second group of texts, joy is contrasted to sorrow, grieving, affliction, distress and the like. Joy (eventually) replaces these other responses, actions, or emotions; or, perhaps better, joy comes because those things that lead to sorrow, those things that cause grief and

---

4. But the pattern is not consistent in the LXX or in the translations of other books. Sixty-five times in the LXX *euphrosynē* translates *śimḥâ*; *chara* appears for *śimḥâ* six times; *agalliama*, three times. *Euphrosynē* also translates several others words, but none so frequently as *śimḥâ* . This analysis could be made more precise by noting that the patterns vary in different books of the LXX to render underlying Hebrew roots. For example, the translator(s) of the Psalms used *euphrainesthai* for *śimḥâ* and *agalliasthai* for *rānan*; but in Isaiah, *euphrainesthai* is used for the Hebrew *rānan* and *agalliasthai* is used for *gîl*. In Stoicism, joy (*chara*) belongs to the right sensibilities (*eupatheiai*), along with volition (*boulēsis*) and precaution (*eulabeia*), that are part of the rightly ordered emotional life (Plutarch, *Virt. mor.* 449B). Diogenes Laertes describes the Stoic understanding of joy as follows: "Joy (*chara*), the counterpart [or, opposite] of pleasure, is rational elation" (DL 7.116).

distress, are removed or taken away. Joy is often anticipated and hoped for as people await those events and circumstances that turn mourning into rejoicing and celebrating. Perhaps most notable is the joy that is anticipated and expected when God acts to redeem and restore his people. This understanding of joy as the appropriate response to God's saving acts, following a period of sorrow or affliction, dominates the pages of the Old Testament.

Yet a third trajectory may also be found in the Scriptures, and more particularly in the New Testament, although the groundwork is laid for it by the eschatological hopes voiced in the prophets. Here, joy (*chara*) is not the experience of elation and celebration that follows affliction and distress, but rather that disposition manifested in the midst of affliction and distress. This joy is or provides a deeply grounded sense of well-being in the present world, even when things in the present world do not seem to be going especially well.

If the first two sets of texts show rejoicing or joy that arises from certain circumstances or events, a *joy because* of the good that one has or experiences, the third kind of joy or rejoicing is a *joy notwithstanding* one's condition, state, or circumstances, joy when one's circumstances seem not to warrant it. But those who have joy even in the midst of distress and affliction have reasons for joy; they are neither sadistic nor masochistic nor glib. In the Scriptures, the person who has *joy notwithstanding* his or her circumstances has faith that suffering and affliction do not signal the absence of God from life or the world. *Joy notwithstanding* also looks forward in hope anticipating the action of God to remove all affliction and tribulation, when the inhabitants of the earth will sing with everlasting joy, because God will have brought about the conditions for it.

"The Trees Clap Their Hands"

First, and briefly, we note a set of texts in which joy, gladness, mirth, and the like are the expected or natural human responses to a variety of occasions, such as festivals, worship, or other occasions associated with the temple activities (Num. 10:10; 2 Sam. 6:12; 1 Chr. 15:16; Ezra 3:12–13; Eccl. 10:19), the naming of a king (1 Kgs. 1:40), weddings (Jer. 25:10), wine (Judg. 9:13; Ps. 104:15; Eccl. 10:19),[5] a good word (Prov. 12:25), wise offspring (Prov. 15:20), or seeing a friend or relative (Exod. 4:14). All such occasions and objects are good things, and in such times or in response to such occasions, people are glad. They rejoice. Perhaps to be included here are those passages where the natural creation—the sun, the pastures, and meadows—act or sing with joy (Pss. 19:5; 65:12–13).[6] In response to the Creator or sovereign God, the natural world responds in joy, even as elsewhere creation is said to do the bidding of the Lord.[7] This response of rejoicing, of singing with joy and gladness, demonstrates that the proper (even "natural") disposition of the world ought to be (and is) that of joy.

There is also in the Scriptures a related, but somewhat different emphasis, namely, that there is joy in the presence of God. In Nehemiah one finds the memorable statement, "The joy of the Lord is your strength" (Neh. 8:10). The structure of the passage suggests

---

5. But heed the warning of Eccl. 2:3, where such enjoyments are deemed foolishness!

6. In Isaiah, the trees rejoice because God has struck down the wicked. As a result, the whole earth "is at rest and quiet" and the trees exult that "no one comes to cut us down'" (Isa. 14:8). Is the point that in God's "peaceable kingdom" there is no destruction of any kind of the natural order? Or no (implied?) misuse of the natural order?

7. According to Sirach, the heavenly bodies "never disobey [God's] word" (16:28). Or, again, Sirach speaks of the natural phenomena of wind, fire, hail, famine, and pestilence as serving the purposes of God: "They take delight in doing his bidding, always ready for his service on earth; and when their time comes they never disobey his command" (39:31; 43:5, 10). Thus the natural phenomena manifest that response to God that human beings ought to offer up. Perhaps the same is true with respect to joy and celebration. If the sun runs its course with joy, and the meadows and valleys shout and sing together for joy, ought not human beings to do so as well?

that "joy of the Lord"[8] probably refers to the human experience and expression of rejoicing ("joy occasioned by the Lord"), since rejoicing is the opposite of weeping. The fact that the day is "holy to our Lord" should occasion "great rejoicing" (Neh. 8:10–12). The note is sounded in the Psalms. The psalmist prays, "Let the light of your face shine on us, O Lord!" and follows that petition with the exclamation, "You have put gladness (*śimḥâ; euphrosynēn*) in my heart more than when their grain and wine abound" (Ps. 4:6–7).

While an abundance of the good things of the earth leads (rightly) to gladness, there is an experience of gladness, a kind of joy that comes from God and exceeds that which is granted by the physical world. So also we read the words of the psalmist: "In your presence there is fullness of joy" (16:11)[9] and "you make [the king] glad with the joy of your presence" (21:6). In both of these cases, "presence" translates the Hebrew word for face (*pāneh*; cf. Ps. 4:6, "your face"). Here too the human experience of joy depends on God's turning his face toward—that is, looking favorably upon—a person (cf. Num. 6:25–26). God's favor brings gladness. God brings gladness. God is not a passive observer of the joy of his people, nor even solely the object of their rejoicing, but the one who brings about that rejoicing and gladness. The author of 1 Chronicles states that honor, majesty, strength, glory, holy splendor, and "joy are in his place" (1 Chr. 16:27–29). Therefore, the heavens are to be glad, the earth is to rejoice, and the nations are to proclaim that the Lord is king (16:30-31). The trees "sing for joy" in the presence of the Lord who judges the earth.[10] "Joy" and "rejoicing" are not merely the "natural"

8. Since the contents of the LXX do not precisely mirror the MT, there are two translations of Neh. 8:10 and hence of the phrase "the joy of the Lord (*ḥedwat yhwh*) is your strength." In both cases, the LXX understands God to be the active agent in bringing about joy or rejoicing.

9. John Goldingay translates "joyful abundance will be with your face," commenting, "When Yhwh's face shines on people, they experience great joy through Yhwh's abundant provision for their needs" (*Psalms 1–41*, Baker Commentary on the Old Testament Wisdom and Psalms, vol. 1 [Grand Rapids: Baker, 2006], 233).

response of the created order to their Creator, but the results of the particular contours of God's activity, namely, God's gracious favor and God's righteous judgment on the earth. It is not "the world" per se that occasions rejoicing, but God's ordering of the world that does so. Thus the bounty of the world elicits joy. The children of Zion rejoice and are glad in the Lord their God because his vindication of them results in the return of the abundance of the land, fruit-bearing trees and vines, vats overflowing with wine and oil (Joel 2:2–24): God's goodness manifests itself in the earth's bounty that leads, in turn, to joy and gladness. And this leads us then to the second cluster of biblical texts.

"Joy Comes in the Morning"

In a number of biblical texts, joy and rejoicing are contrasted with sorrow, grieving, mourning, and the like. Hence we read in the Psalms, "Weeping may linger for the night, but joy comes with the morning" (MT Ps. 30:6, *rinnâ* ["ringing cry, jubilation"], LXX *agalliasis*). Later in the same Psalm, we read, "You have turned my mourning into dancing, and clothed me with joy" (MT Ps. 30:12, *śimḥâ*; LXX 29:12, *euphrosynēn*). Weeping and mourning are replaced with dancing and joy; they are not experienced simultaneously. In Psalm 51, the penitent sinner prays, "Let me hear joy and gladness; let the bones that you have crushed rejoice" (51:8; *śāśón wĕśimḥâ*; *agalliasin kai euphrosynēn*). In this prayer, the psalmist anticipates or hopes for a turn of events so that he will be able to rejoice. Indeed, he depends on God to act favorably so that he may rejoice. Thus

---

10. In 1 Chr. 16:27–31, the usual range and variety of Hebrew and Greek words are found, with one exception: in 1 Chr. 16:27, the LXX translates the Hebrew *ḥedwâ* ("joy") as *kauchēma* ("boasting"). William Morrice defines *kauchasthai* as "joyful boasting," and includes the word group in his study of joy in the New Testament, but his attachment of the adjective *joyful* to "boasting" arises from his theological reading that Paul's is a proper boasting when contrasted to misdirected Jewish boasting.

he prays, "Restore to me the joy of your salvation" (v. 12). He does not rejoice at present because his current distress is due to God's punishment for his sin; thus he can only turn to God in repentance and beg God for relief. There can be no rejoicing for the psalmist until God turns his face again toward the penitent (Ps. 51:9, 11–12), until God delivers him (v. 14). Indeed, in the present situation it would be inappropriate to rejoice, because the psalmist suffers because of his own guilt and the just punishment of God. Thus he hopes for God's deliverance and restoration, and trusts in God's grace and kindness. So also when in captivity in Babylon, the exiles lay down and wept: they did not sing the songs of Zion (Ps. 137:1–4). Only when the Lord restores the fortunes of Zion does one laugh, rejoice, and shout for joy (Ps. 126:1–2; cf. Pss. 14:7; 40:16; 70:4; 90:14; 118:24; Isa. 9:3, 25:9; Matt. 5:12).

Similarly, Isaiah describes the period of God's punishment, of exile, or of tyranny, evil, or injustice, as a time characterized by the lack of joy, gladness, and rejoicing (16:10; 22:13; 24:11; 29:19–21; 35:1-2). Times of desolation are just that, and they are not characterized by joy or gladness; indeed, given that in the prophets these times are (often) brought about by God because of Israel's disobedience, it would be inappropriate to rejoice and be glad.[11] But when God breaks the yoke of the oppressor, the people rejoice (9:3). Acknowledging God's salvation, God's bringing just judgment upon the earth, and the presence of the Holy One of Israel among them, the people sing for joy (12:3, 6; cf. 24:14; 26:19; 29:19; 35:2, 6; cf. Zech. 2:10). Especially notable is Isaiah's repeated description of the return of the "ransomed of the Lord" to Zion: "everlasting joy" shall be on their heads (35:10; 51:11; 61:7). God will comfort Zion, and

---

11. It is therefore also wrong for the wicked to rejoice because of the troubles of the righteous (Judg. 16:23; Ps. 35:15) or to rejoice in foolishness (Prov. 15:21). Not only will such joy end, but inasmuch as it runs counter to God's purposes, it must end.

"joy and gladness" will be found in her (51:3). Isaiah's vision of the future includes the experience of joy and peace (55:12). And, finally, those who love Jerusalem are exhorted to rejoice and, indeed, to "rejoice with joy" or "rejoice greatly."[12]

As is the case with other books of the Old Testament, the familiar New Testament word for joy or rejoice (*chara, chairō*) appears only rarely in the Septuagint version of Isaiah. But Isaiah describes the response to God's activity of deliverance and restoration as that of rejoicing, anticipating its persistence by describing it as "everlasting joy." Perhaps not surprisingly, then, the realm of future wholeness and salvation can be pictured as marked by joy and peace, the state of affairs that corresponds to the time when God removes all causes of sorrow, wiping away every tear, and when the peoples beat their swords into plowshares. Isaiah would find it difficult to separate the "inner state of joy" from its "external expression," and both from the concrete act of salvation that has brought them about. The coming era of joy is a time when people rejoice, that is, they offer thanksgiving and praise to God, to celebrate God's justice and deliverance of his people.

Thus however we might define joy, we note the striking fact that in the Scriptures of both the Old and New Testaments, God's actions are the cause of and reason for joy and rejoicing.[13] Even God joins in the rejoicing. "On that day" in which God restores "the remnant of Israel," removing the judgments passed against it, not only is Israel to rejoice, but the Lord himself "will exult over you with joy" and "rejoice over you with loud singing" (Zeph. 3:16-17, translation

---

12. The Greek word *chara* that figures so importantly in the NT is found in LXX Isa. 55:12 and 66:10 (*charēte chara*; 66:10). Elsewhere the word typically rendered joy in the NRSV is *euphrosynē* (35:10; 51:3, 11; and 61:7).

13. According to 1QM, the army of God carries banners into war that read, among other things, "God's battle," "God's revenge," "God's lawsuit," and "God's might." When they return from battle, presumably victorious, their banners read, "God's acts of salvation," "God's victory," "God's help," and "God's joy" (1QM 4:12–14).

altered).[14] God celebrates his own acts of salvation by celebrating the people who have been saved. And by rejoicing in their deliverance, they are in turn both rejoicing in God's act and sharing in God's celebration of it. This rejoicing focuses on what God has done and on the changed situation of the one who has been delivered and who therefore rejoices, on the movement from judgment (of or by God) to deliverance (by God) from the consequences of that judgment. In the same vein, we read in Nehemiah that upon the return of the exiles to Jerusalem, the people "offered great sacrifices that day and rejoiced, for God had made them rejoice with great joy; the women and children also rejoiced. The joy of Jerusalem was heard far away" (Neh. 12:43). Particularly interesting here is the verb "God had made them rejoice." The point is that what God has done has led to their rejoicing: God's action (of restoration, of deliverance) is the cause of their rejoicing. Similarly, but on an individual rather than corporate level, the psalmist prays that God will restore the "joy of your salvation."[15] Joy, or rejoicing, is the proper response to, and occasioned by, God's saving activity.[16]

Certainly in the NT one finds the picture of the God who rejoices over the restoration and return of those who are brought into the realm of God's salvation. In the parable of the lost sheep (Luke

14. In this passage, the words translated "joy" and "rejoice" come from *śimḥâ* and cognates, translated in the LXX with *euphrosynē* and cognates. Morrice notes, but does not develop, the point that the joy (*euphrosynē*) of God's people "is matched by joy in the heart of God himself" (*Joy in the New Testament*, 27). The Jewish exegete and philosopher, Philo, wrote that "to rejoice belongs to God alone," because God is free from grief, fear, and suffering, "the only nature that possesses complete happiness and blessedness" (*eudaimonias kai makaristētos; Abr.* 202). So also *Cher.* 86, where God alone rejoices because God alone is free from pain and fear, does not participate in evil, does not suffer sorrow or fatigue, and enjoys peace untainted by war. In other words, God now enjoys what human beings yearn for (*Cher.* 87).

15. In Neh. 12:43, again the Greek words for joy and rejoicing again come from *euphrainō* and cognates, translating the Hebrew *śimḥâ* and cognates. In Ps. 51.12, the Greek word translated "joy" is *agalliasin;* the Hebrew is *śāśôn.* As noted previously, the NT word *chara* is rare in the LXX.

16. One could perhaps quibble whether "the joy of salvation" refers to the joy one has in or because of God's salvation or the joy that comes from that salvation. Given the fact that "salvation" requires an action of God, the difference between these types of genitives is rendered moot.

15:4-7), Jesus speaks of a shepherd who goes in search of one lost sheep, rejoices (*chairōn*) when he finds it, and calls his friends to rejoice with him (*syncharēte moi*), and then compares that shepherd's joy to the "joy in heaven" (*chara en tō ouranō*) if one sinner repents. The same notes are sounded in the parable about the woman who lost but found one of her ten silver coins. In this parable, however, we read that there is joy "in the presence of the angels of God" (15:10). Those who are with God, who are in God's presence, celebrate the finding of the lost. Even as God rejoices in his own action of delivering the exiles out of captivity, so the shepherd rejoices in his own action of finding what is his own, and invites others to celebrate with him; the woman rejoices in her own action of finding what is her own, and invites others to celebrate with her (15:10). But the appropriate response to God's expected deliverance is found already in the opening chapters of the Gospel. When the angel Gabriel informs Zechariah of the coming birth of John, he notes that Zechariah "will have joy and gladness" (*estai chara soi kai agalliasis*), and that many will rejoice (*charēsontai*) at John's birth (1:14).[17] This promise is magnified when a host of angels announce to the shepherds a "great joy" (*charan megalēn*) that will be for "all people" (*panti tō laō*).[18] Indeed, the joy that characterizes God's response to the finding of the lost—their return to God and the people of God—ought to characterize the response of all people to

---

17. Jesus "rejoiced in the Holy Spirit" upon learning of the triumphs of the seventy as they returned from their mission (Luke 10:21); the early church met together, receiving their food "with rejoicing" (*en agalliasei*; cf. Luke 16:34). Defining *agalliasis* and various cognates as "exultant joy," Morrice speaks also of it as eschatological joy that can be anticipated in faith (*Joy in the New Testament*, 23). That meaning belongs not to the word itself, but rather to the contexts in which it is used.

18. It may be noted here that, whatever other words Luke uses, he does tend to prefer and use the common NT word for joy and its cognates, namely, *chara*. On the whole, this is the pattern of the NT, but not the LXX.

that salvation. Not only do they receive the benefits of God's gracious deliverance, but in doing so they share God's own response to it.

This point is made in Matthew in the parable of the talents. When the master rewards the servants who have been "good and faithful" he invites them to "enter into the joy" of their master (*eiselthe eis tēn charan tou kyriou sou*; Matt. 25:21, 23, translation altered). Is "the joy of your master" the joy that the master has, a personal joy ("I am joyful")? Or is it the kind of joy that the master can bring about or give ("I have joy for you")? It is interesting to substitute different words in the invitation to "enter into the joy" of the master. One could, for example, be invited to enter into the house, inheritance, family, or kingdom of the master. To enter into the "joy" of the master implies sharing the master's own response to something, the master's own elation. The master rejoices over the faithful, and in turn the faithful may rejoice—enter into the master's joy—as well.

"Rejoice in the Lord Always"

This leads us, then, to the third trajectory found in the Scriptures. The future-looking hopes we identified as part of the second biblical cluster of texts regarding joy and rejoicing lay the groundwork for understanding joy as that attitude experienced or expressed in times of affliction and suffering. The word used here is typically, although not exclusively, *chara*, and its chief representative is Paul. To be sure, there are places in Paul's writings where sorrow or grief stand in contrast to joy. For example, Paul writes to the Corinthians with the hope he will not have sorrow but joy (2 Cor. 2:3). Yet later in the same letter Paul speaks warmly of the abundance of joy manifested by the churches of Macedonia during "a severe ordeal of affliction," a joy that overflowed in generosity (2 Cor. 8:2; cf. 7:4-16). Those churches include the believers in Thessaloniki, whom Paul describes having "received the word with joy inspired by the Holy Spirit" (1 Thess. 1:6), as well as the believers of Philippi.

The letter to the Philippians may be the Pauline epistle in which joy plays its most prominent role (1:4, 18, 25; 2:2, 17, 18, 28, 29; 3:1; 4:1, 4, 10). Although penned while he was imprisoned and uncertain about the outcome of his imprisonment and whether he would live or die, Paul here writes that even if he is "being poured out as a libation," he remains glad and rejoices, and calls on the Philippians also to rejoice with him (2:17-18). Paul also exhorts them, "Rejoice in the Lord always; again I will say, Rejoice" (4:4; cf. 3:1; 4:10). In the context of the letter, this exhortation is preceded by the famous "Christ hymn" (2:5-11), in which Paul recounts the path of Jesus: he who was in the form of God emptied himself, humbled himself, and was obedient even unto death; it is this one whom God has exalted and honored. It is this Jesus whom Paul yearns to know, both to share in his sufferings even unto death and to experience the power of resurrection from the dead (3:10-11; Col. 1:24). To share in suffering is to share the very life of Christ. Elsewhere Paul also plots the course and significance of his own life along that of Jesus' life, the one to whom he is joined in dying and rising, in life and in death (Rom. 6:3–11; 14:7-9; 2 Cor. 4:9-10).

Paul's joy, then, is a *joy notwithstanding* the circumstances of his imprisonment and affliction, because he has faith that he is sharing in the sufferings of his Lord and hope that he will share in Christ's resurrection. Even as Paul's identity is now reconfigured by and through the one who loved him and gave himself for him (Gal. 2:20; Eph 5:2, 25), so Paul's joy is occasioned by his participation in the death and resurrection of Jesus. His conviction that he is joined to Christ in his suffering, and the hope that he will be joined to Christ in his resurrection, converge to give him joy in his present dismal circumstances. In that sense, *joy notwithstanding* is indeed a joy *because of*, that is, joy because Paul is joined precisely *in* his suffering to the Lord Jesus Christ who "will transform the body of our humiliation that it may be conformed to the body of his glory" (Phil. 3:21). In suffering and in vindication, in death and in life, "whether we live or whether we die, we are the Lord's" (Rom. 14:8).

Other authors of the New Testament also write of having joy in the midst of trials—indeed, even of the possibilities that trials produce joy. Notable in this regard are both the epistles of James and 1 Peter, with similar exhortations: "Whenever you face trials of any kind, consider it nothing but joy" (James 1:2); "In this you rejoice, even if now for a little while you have had to suffer various trials" (1 Pet. 1:6). In both cases, it is the result in view that allows for joy in the present. The testing of faith brought about by trials of various sorts leads to endurance and maturity (James 1:3-4), or to the manifestation of the genuineness of one's faith, itself revealed finally in the outcome or result of that faith, namely, salvation (1 Pet. 1:6-9). There is joy not because one is afflicted, but because affliction can serve to test and establish one's faithfulness, and that results, in the end, in salvation. The passage from 1 Peter also emphasizes the pointedly personal and finally inexpressible aspect of "joy." Here the author addresses his readers by reminding them that although they have not seen Jesus Christ in the present, they love him and have faith in him, and "rejoice with an indescribable and glorious joy" (*agalliasthe charai aneklalētōi kai dedoxasmenē*). They do so because they are anticipating their salvation, thus looking forward in hope, and that hope reaches back into the present to give "indescribable and glorious joy."

Especially the second and third biblical trajectories discussed here are found in the Gospel of John. On the one hand, joy vanquishes sorrow; the two do not exist simultaneously. Anticipating his death and departure from the disciples, Jesus warns them that they will "weep and mourn" while the world rejoices, but then assures them that their sorrow will turn "into joy" (*eis charan*; 16:20) because they will see him again and, at that time, "no one will take your joy from you" (16:22). The warning about the disciples' imminent sorrow and subsequent joy refer, in the first place, to responses to Jesus' death and resurrection. The disciples will grieve and mourn because Jesus will be killed; they will rejoice when they see him, because that will indicate both that Jesus is alive and that he is now with the Father. He has completed his mission and returned to the Father who sent him. Not only may the disciples rejoice because Jesus' mission has not been in vain, having in fact accomplished that which the Father has sent him to do, but because he has returned to the Father from whom he came and with whom he is one. His presence there insures his return to the disciples. But his presence there also insures his ongoing presence with the disciples. Their initial sorrow arises from Jesus' absence; their joy is elicited by his presence.[19]

The joy of the disciples is described in distinctive terms as "fulfilled" (or "completed") joy (15:11; 16:24; 17:13). As a result of their union with Christ, being joined to him as branches are to the vine, the disciples glorify God, abide in the love of the Father and Son, and keep their commandments. This way of living that begins with "abiding" in Christ, or in the love of the Father and the Son, issues in keeping the commandment to love. And that reality expresses itself further in joy (15:11). Furthermore, the union of the believer with Christ in and through his love is such that they receive what they ask

---

19. At this point, John is notoriously difficult. Exactly when and how Jesus will be "present" with his disciples has generated significant discussion. Indeed, one could argue that the entire problem dealt with in the Farewell Discourses is the problem that Jesus will be absent from the disciples. The various promises—to come and take them to be with them; to send the Spirit; to dwell with and among them—serve to mitigate the reality of Jesus' absence, while at the same time acknowledging that he is not now with them as he was. So the "joy" that the disciples have, even when he is raised and appears to them, always remains forward looking to that time when they will be with him. For the promise that Jesus will be with them, see 14:27-28, 15:4-5; Jesus will take them to be with him in the Father's house, 14:2-3; that Jesus and the Father will be with them, 14:19, 23; and that the Spirit will be with them, 14:17, 26; 15:26; 16:7, 13.

for in order that their joy may be completed (16:24). The relationship of believers to the Father through the Son has as its destiny the full participation in the joy that he gives them. This is his own joy, the joy that comes from him and that characterizes the one who fully accomplishes the will of the Father. Furthermore, the joy that Jesus gives them is a joy that they possess even now, while "in the world" (17:13), and in spite of the fact that the world hates them and even persecutes them (17:14; 15:11-20). In the midst of their trying circumstances, they have comfort, courage, and peace (14:1, 27) because they can be assured both of the presence of their Lord with them in the midst of their trials, and of the hope that they will be with him, where he is—and that their presence with him in the Father's house will bring an end to their distress.

But already the Baptist had announced that he "rejoices greatly" (*chara chairei*) and that his joy has been "fulfilled" at the coming of the bridegroom (3:29). This image of Jesus as the bridegroom may reflect the portrayal of God as the bridegroom of Israel in the Old Testament (Isa. 62:5; Jer. 3:20; Ezek. 16:32; Hos. 1:2; 2:2; and see Eph. 5:23-32). If God's judgment on Israel can be portrayed quite concretely as bringing an end to the joy of a bride and bridegroom (Jer. 7:34; 16:9; 25:10; 33:11), then with the coming of the Messiah, the bridegroom, and the time of God's salvation, it is time to rejoice. Once again, God brings about the conditions that occasion joy. John writes later, "The reaper is already receiving wages and is gathering fruit for eternal life, so that sower and reaper may rejoice together" (4:36). The reaper overtakes the sower; this is the overlap of the time that is coming with the time that "now is" (cf. 4:21, 23; 5:25, 28). And that convergence of fulfillment in the present but anticipation of the future explains also the experience of eschatological joy in the present while yet hoping for the arrival of those conditions that bring joy to all the earth and its inhabitants.

Joy is therefore forward looking; it is linked with hope; it characterizes the coming and inbreaking kingdom of God (cf. Rom. 12:12; 15:13). That joy is forward looking coheres with and is an outgrowth of the biblical expectation that God's judgments on the earth bring about righteousness. As noted earlier, a significant strand of biblical thought associates joy with God's deliverance because that signals either release from oppression and injustice, or that God has now turned with favor toward his people once more. When the acceptable year of the Lord has come, it is appropriate to rejoice. There can be no joy over injustice, even if the Bible will also bear witness to those who experience joy while and in the midst of suffering. Joy characterizes those who have experienced God's deliverance because they celebrate God's righteousness and justice. As the psalmist exclaims, "Let those who desire my vindication shout for joy and be glad, and say evermore, 'Great is the Lord, who delights in the welfare of his servant'" (Ps. 35:27; cf. 32:11). Because the Lord judges with equity, the nations sing for joy (Ps. 37:4).[20] Joy therefore also belongs to those who anticipate God's deliverance, God's righteousness, and God's justice. Those who live between the times of God's graciousness toward his people and the world in the past and the anticipation of them in the future have joy because they trust in a reality that transcends the world's horizons, but that will effect the goodness of the world. At present, what they see can elicit only a partial joy that anticipates the fullness of God's remaking of the world; thus both faith and hope are necessary concomitants of joy.

Not surprisingly, joy belongs to the fruit of the Spirit, to those human qualities and dispositions that the Spirit of God effects and that ought to characterize not only the individual but the community

---

20. The expressions of celebration because of the victories in battle and the triumphs over one's enemies granted by God (1 Sam. 18:6; 2 Chr. 20:27) can only be short-lived; joy must be coupled with peace and righteousness.

together (Gal. 5:22; Acts 15:32). Many of the fruits of the Spirit can really only be exercised in community, that is, with an eye toward the other. Love, patience, kindness, and generosity, for example, are not merely inner states of being, but how one lives with respect to the other. What, then, of joy? Paul does invite others to rejoice with him, and speaks of Christians sharing in joy (1 Cor. 12:26; 13:6; Phil. 2:18; cf. 1:25; 2:2; Philem. 7). Looking back to the Old Testament, one can also note that frequently calls to rejoice are addressed to the people as a whole. For example, in Deuteronomy the people are called to rejoice on the occasion of festivals and when going to the temple, and they are called to rejoice in the company of others, a point underscored by their gathering together in the central sanctuary. Rejoicing is the activity and response of the people together.[21] While joy can at times characterize the disposition of the individual,[22] particularly in times of affliction, it also denotes that conduct or way of life that belongs to God's people when they are in the proper relationship to God. In other words, "joy" is not a coping mechanism for dealing with difficulty, but the way one lives with others and before God.

Summary Reflections

As was noted frequently above, "joy" and "rejoicing" are most typically—indeed, almost always—lodged in the cultic sphere, in worship, or in the experience of the presence of God or the acknowledgment of the divine saving activity of God. So, from one perspective, we can say that God creates the conditions for joy, and that, therefore, God is finally responsible for human joy and

---

21. "You and your households together," Deut. 12:7, 14:26; "you and your sons and your daughters, your male and female slaves, the Levites resident in your towns, as well as the strangers, the orphans, and the widows who are among you," 16:11; cf. 26:11.

22. In the OT joy is associated with the heart (Exod. 4:14; Pss. 19:8, 104:15; Prov. 15:30) or the soul (Ps. 86:4).

human flourishing. This is the witness of the biblical texts: when God restores the fortunes of Zion, then there is rejoicing; when the shepherd finds the one sheep that was lost, then all are to rejoice; when God brings his sovereign rule to bear on the earth, then there is "righteousness, peace, and joy in the Holy Spirit." We may, then, legitimately charge God with the responsibility of bringing those conditions on earth that make possible, even necessary, the human response of joy. This responsibility is the outgrowth of God's identity as the Creator of all that is, or at least of God's identity as the good Creator of all that is good. Joy is therefore the human response to God's establishing, whether in creation or final redemption, a good world in which people find *shalom*. As part of human flourishing, joy is thus linked to, and dependent upon, participation in the world of God's creation and its re-creation. If joy is response to God's activity, God's deliverance, joy may be experienced by those who neither see nor discern God's deliverance, but it is deepened by gratitude that discerns the hand of God at work for good.

Since joy is often that emotion or response that follows or replaces sorrow and distress, joy (rejoicing, gladness) is caused or effected by external circumstances or events. It is not appropriate to rejoice at oppression or tyranny or sorrow. Weeping is not rejoicing, but it will be turned to rejoicing. This does not mean that joy is fickle, but rather that joy is the response to the goodness of the order of the world. What is good elicits joy. The Scriptures thus indicate that genuine joy is linked with righteousness and peace, and that all these together depend upon God's action to bring them about. The world does not on its own do justice or establish righteousness; it cannot, therefore, effect the circumstances that make for human joy. Because it responds to the good in the world, joy is therefore not indifference; it is not immune to the vagaries of human existence. Joy may disappear when there is great tragedy or loss; it will return when things are set to rights, when the causes of tragedy are taken away. Throughout the biblical accounts, joy is a response to events, elicited by God's salvation, by various triumphs, and so on. Paul experienced joy in the midst of suffering because he understood it to be a sharing in Christ's suffering, thus anticipating participation in Christ's resurrection. Suffering that has no end does not elicit joy.

Thus while the authors of the Bible hope for the time when they will be able to rejoice fully, they also rejoice in the present; they experience joy and gladness; they know of life that is characterized by equanimity, gratitude, and celebration, even if part of a life not untainted by war, injustice, conflict, debilitating illness, or death. The joy that is experienced in the present, prior to the removal of all causes of sorrow, acknowledges both the goodness of God's bountiful world and anticipates the outpouring of God's full blessings in the future. When Paul calls people to rejoice in the Lord always, the key may be the focus on "the Lord." One does not always rejoice in the world, or in circumstances; but one may rejoice in the Lord. To cultivate this trust and confidence in God and God's goodness is to cultivate joy.

Such scriptural statements raise the question about how we should characterize joy; that is, is it a virtue? habit? emotion? attitude? Joy seems to arise spontaneously from the good things of the world: from wine, weddings, children, worship, or victory. As such, it is perhaps best classified as an emotion. Joy is effusive; joyful people celebrate, sing, clap, and shout. But joy can also be commanded. Indeed, Paul even commands the Philippians to rejoice in the Lord always. Joy is not simply or only the natural response to events, but can be commanded. Joy is therefore closer to a way of living that arises from being "in the Lord" and in turn rejoices in that identity. It is a counterintuitive response to the world. If the rest of the context of Philippians were taken into account, joy would be the disposition that accompanies the one who presses on toward the prize; who, forgetting what lies behind, strains toward what lies ahead (3:13-14.) Joy cannot be severed from hope and may even be said to arise or be possible precisely because one has hope. Even as joy is expressed when God brings about salvation, so joy may be known prior to that time because one anticipates God's salvation in hope. But where there is no hope, it is doubtful that there can be joy.

In sum, then, on the one hand, joy is brought about or occasioned by circumstances. It appropriately celebrates that which is good, righteous and just. Joy is joy because it understands and responds to that which God desires for the world—wholeness, abundance, justice, peace. Joy is therefore a response to external circumstances, and is shaped by them. Joy is the appropriate response to the well-being of God's world. Joy therefore expresses itself in singing, shouting, celebration; it is an effusive emotional response. Joy reflects God's own rejoicing in the world and its goodness. Because joy celebrates the goodness of God and God's world, it is therefore also appropriately disturbed when the well-being of God's world is interrupted or disturbed.

But, on the other hand, precisely because joy is grounded in the expectation of God's deliverance, it has the character of perseverance, confidence, and trust. It is not the same as perseverance, but neither is it fickle. Joy is reoriented in the New Testament around the initial fulfillment of that hope in God's saving work in Christ. Joy is thus both a response to God's salvation in Christ, and the attitude or disposition in the present time that is based on a confidence in God's goodness and gracious disposition toward humankind. In this sense, then, joy cannot be disturbed by external circumstances, even while—or, perhaps because—it anticipates that day when God wipes away every tear from every eye. Joy is a disposition that anticipates a time when all that destroys human well-being, the *shalom* of the world and its inhabitants, will be removed. Joy is a way of living that hopes for God's final *shalom* but, anticipating that *shalom* already in the present, also lives with confident hope and gratitude in the present time. Joy is the effusive expression of gratitude and praise that flows from a resolute, trusting heart that is suffused by hope in God.

3

Joy: Some New Testament Perspectives and Questions

N.T. Wright

Every year in the church's calendar we read the story of Jesus' ascension in Acts 1. But we also remind ourselves of the much shorter version of the same story that Luke has placed at the end of his Gospel (24:50–53). There we find a phrase that has always puzzled me. Jesus, says Luke, was separated from them and carried up into heaven; whereupon they worshiped him, and returned to Jerusalem "with great joy." This seems, to put it mildly, counterintuitive. Why would they be so joyful if Jesus has been taken from them? Ought they not to be sorrowful? Might not his departure signal the start of danger, of fear, of the loss of a sense of direction? What is this "joy" that they now have? What is the reason for it—either in the original historical setting, or in Luke's vision, as he writes these books a few decades later?

This problem, to be sure, is noticed in the New Testament itself. The Fourth Gospel anticipates it in the so-called Farewell Discourses, when Jesus explains that he is going away, and that this will cause his followers great sadness—but that the sadness will be replaced with joy. "So you have pain now; but I will see you again, and your hearts will rejoice, and no one will take your joy from you" (John 16:22). This finds an obvious echo in the resurrection narrative, when Jesus appears in the upper room, and "the disciples rejoiced when they saw the Lord" (20:20). And yet in John's Gospel, as well as in Luke, the obvious sense of joy at seeing Jesus alive again after his crucifixion does not seem to get to the heart of the "joy" of which Jesus speaks in the discourses. He speaks of "the ruler of this world" who is "coming," and who is to be "driven out" (12:31; 14:30), and in that light tells his followers that, though they will have trouble in the world, they are to cheer up, because "I have conquered the world" (16:33). The joy that the disciples have at Jesus' resurrection, and at the prospect of his ascension (14:28), is therefore not simply the human delight at discovering a dead friend and master to be alive again. John is pointing his readers to a deeper meaning, having to do with the world itself. Something is happening—something has happened—as a result of which the world is a different place. That is the ultimate reason for the disciples' joy, a joy resting on a foundation that, it seems, no trouble or sorrow can shake.

It has been easy in modern Western Christianity to characterize this "joy" in terms of human emotions. One might obviously link it either to the "romantic" Christian movements that have reacted against rationalism (a notable example being C. S. Lewis's famous autobiography, *Surprised by Joy*), or to the "charismatic" movements that have brought new energy to staid or static mainline churches, both Protestant and Catholic. To be sure, it would be bizarre to think or speak of "joy" while bracketing out the sense of human delight, elation, and celebration that for most people is the simple meaning of the word. Yet in the New Testament the "joy" and "rejoicing" that forms such a common theme is capable of overlapping with quite different human emotions. Paul can instruct the Philippians to "rejoice in the Lord always" while at the same time speaking of the possibility, had his friend Epaphroditus died of his illness, that he himself would have had "one sorrow after another" (Phil. 4:4 with 2:27). Something different from "ordinary" human joy, even exceptional but still "ordinary" joy, seems to be envisaged here. In Philippians, as in Luke and John, it has to do with "the Lord," who for Paul is the risen and ascended Jesus of Philippians 2:9-11 and 3:20-21. I shall return to this.

But if the "joy" to which the New Testament summons its readers is of a different order to that of regular, even exceptional, human experience, it is also different—so it seems to me—from the mood of the Jewish world of the Second Temple period. It presents a fresh retrieval of the joy that is a frequent note in Israel's Scriptures. To make this point, we need to look briefly at the theme of joy in the Scriptures, and then in the world of the Second Temple period.

"Joy" in Israel's Scriptures and Beyond

A quick read through Israel's Scriptures would reveal "joy" as a significant theme with very specific connotations. Sometimes, of course, the reality is present without the word (we must always remind ourselves of the danger of the concordance!): an obvious example is the song of wild delight sung by Miriam and the rest in Exodus 15. It is a celebration of the power and victory of Israel's God. *Something has happened* as a result of which a new world has opened up. The thing that has happened is simultaneously an act of "judgment" and an act of "rescue." God has acted to put things right, to put a stop to evil, and to deliver his people from their enslaving enemy. The major festivals, particularly Passover, look back to the same act of judgment and deliverance, and their celebration draws meaning from this original act.

One thinks, in the same way, of David dancing before the Lord as the Philistines are defeated and the ark is brought into Jerusalem (2 Samuel 5 and 6). The death of Uzzah prompts a brief pause, but then the celebration begins again (6:6-11, 12-15). David's exuberance draws a sneering rebuke from Saul's daughter (6:16, 20-23), as extravagant celebration often does (compare John 12:1-8!). But the celebration has something of the same flavor as that of Miriam. The enemy has been defeated, a new day is dawning, and Israel's God is showing his powerful presence.

These celebrations also reveal the robustly *physical* nature of "joy" in the Hebrew Scriptures. Celebration will include music, dancing, food and wine, and the giving of presents to one and all (2 Sam. 6:18-19). All are to share in the celebratory feasts, including orphans, widows, and foreigners (Deut. 14:29; 16:11, 14; 26:11). Indeed, right through the Bible the idea of a great feast is one of the central ways in which joy is expressed in a family or community. As we think about biblical joy we are thus led to think about the *reasons for* joy and the *character of* joy. The reasons include a mighty act of God to bring about victory over evil and the rescue of God's people from its grip. The character of joy includes the vigorous and vibrant celebration of the goodness of the created order, expressed through the activities that signal and symbolize human well-being—eating, drinking, the joy of marriage, music and dancing.

Perhaps the most obvious location of "joy" in the Hebrew (and Aramaic) Scriptures is the promise and then the (partial?) reality of the restoration after the Babylonian exile. We think of the mingled joy and weeping as the second temple was founded (Ezra 3:10-13), and the celebrations when the city wall was dedicated (Neh. 12:43, which says, remarkably, that "the joy of Jerusalem was heard far away"; joy was not simply a shared *feeling*; it was something that could be *heard*, from a long way off). Or, with the psalm: "When the Lord restored the fortunes of Zion, we were like those who dream. Then our mouth was filled with laughter, and our tongue with shouts of joy. . . . The Lord has done great things for us, and we rejoiced." This note of *retrospective* joy then turns into a prayer for *fresh* acts of deliverance: "May those who sow in tears reap with shouts of joy. Those who go out weeping, bearing the seed for sowing, shall come home with shouts of joy, carrying their sheaves" (Ps. 126:1-3, 5-6). This too highlights the close link between national and political fortunes (the main subject of the psalm) and the agricultural basis of national life, with the latter thus serving both as metaphor and as metonymy for the restoration of Israel's fortunes.

We find something similar in Isaiah 9: "You have multiplied the nation, you have increased its joy; they rejoice before you as with joy at the harvest, as people exult when dividing plunder" (Isa. 9:3). Here the simile of harvest points on to the new Davidic kingdom of justice and righteousness, in which the animal kingdom will cease from violence and bloodshed (11:1-10). These images are picked up in later portions of the book, as the whole creation celebrates Israel's return from exile: "You shall go out in joy, and be led back in peace; the mountains and the hills before you shall burst into song, and all the trees of the field shall clap their hands" (55:12). In the great coming restoration, Israel's God himself will be rejoicing (62:5; 65:19; compare Ps. 104:31; Deut. 30:9; Zeph. 3:17). "Do not be grieved," say Ezra and Nehemiah to the returning exiles as they hear the Torah, "for the joy of the Lord is your strength" (Neh. 8:10). They then copy David, feasting and drinking and sending portions to those who have nothing. The end of Isaiah also provides another classic statement of Exodus-like joy: "You shall see, and your heart shall rejoice; your bodies [lit.: 'bones'] shall flourish like the grass; and it shall be known that the hand of the Lord is with his servants, and his indignation is against his enemies" (66:14). The great divine action that produces victory over evil and rescue for God's people will be a mixture of new covenant (restoration after exile) and new creation (fresh harvests, producing bodily restoration); and both will cause joy. Indeed—though there are many ways of saying the same thing at this point—one could say that the *covenantal* actions of Israel's God produce *creational* results. History and harvest go closely together. God's actions on behalf of his people will result in the renewal of the good creation. Elements of the latter can serve both as literary metaphors and appropriate celebrations for the former.

All this biblical material remained of course very much in the minds of Second Temple Jews. The Scriptures, and particularly the Psalms, were the soil in which there grew to full flower all later expectations, aspirations, celebrations, and lamentations. The great festivals continued to express and reinforce the celebration of God's powerful deeds in days gone by. But now new elements were added. The "return from exile" was a mixed blessing. Those who had returned to Jerusalem still had a sense of being "enslaved"; the full reality promised in Isaiah 40–55 or Ezekiel 36–45 had not come about. Daniel 9, a passage much discussed in the post-Maccabean period, spoke of the exile lasting not for seventy years but for 490. In particular, though the temple had been rebuilt, there remained a sense that the promise of glorious divine return (Isaiah 40, 52; Ezekiel 43) had not yet happened. It remained in the future (Hag. 2:7; Zech. 2:4-5, 10-11; Mal. 3:1). Indeed, when the rabbis, much later, discussed the ways in which the Second Temple was deficient when compared with the first, one of the key elements missing from the second temple was the Shekinah itself (*b. Yoma 21b*). The joy of geographical return, and of the restoration of cult, was mixed with a sense that something remained incomplete. (We may exempt Ben Sirach from this; there, we do seem to find a grand celebration, with the high priest in the temple and everything seeming to be right with the world. But we have good reason to suppose that this priestly and aristocratic perspective, and such "joy" as it brought, was not widely shared.)

What we find in the Second Temple period, then, is a rich mixture of celebration and expectation. Joy was still expressed in the traditional ways, and for the traditional reasons—with the added reason of the return itself, such as it was, and then the major new reason of the Maccabean triumph, resulting in the institution of a new feast, Hanukkah, and the vivid and evocative joy of the ceremony of the light. But the ambiguities of the postexilic settlement, and the yet more complicated ambiguities of the post-Maccabean period, meant that the joy itself had an increasingly forward look. The Hasmonean monarchy, the Roman invasion, and the rise of Herod and his family, could not prevent the annual celebrations, the joyful recounting of the kingship of God as expressed in the Psalms and elsewhere. But they ensured that this celebration was inevitably more about expectation than about present triumph. The more Daniel 9 was woven into popular consciousness (and this seems to be what Josephus means when he speaks of "an oracle in their scriptures" that drove the people to revolt in the reign of Nero [*Jewish War* 6.312–315]), the more we must conclude that the dominant note of the Second Temple Jewish worldview was not so much joy as hope. A joyful hope, yes, often; but a hope deferred so long, and dashed so repeatedly, that in many texts we find hope in the form of a gritted-teeth determination to hold on at all costs, rather than an easy or cheerful celebration of the fact that what God did in the past he would soon do once more. And when we reach the post-70 period, in books like *4 Ezra* and *2 Baruch*, hope itself has been under severe threat. It is still there, a function as always of creational monotheism (if there is one God, then despite all appearances he *must* eventually act to set things right); but these books have little of the joy of Isaiah 40–55, or of Psalms 96, 98, and 126.

This is not, of course, a criticism. One might as well criticize a young widow for failing to sing cheerful songs at the funeral of her wise and loving husband. But it poses a sharp question when we remind ourselves that the first followers of Jesus were speaking, at exactly the same period, of a "joy" that retained the shape and content of the Jewish phenomenon at which we have glanced, but that had sprung to life in a new and unexpected manner.

Joy in the New Testament

Twenty years ago, I conducted a thought experiment using the worldview model (one particular variation within the contemporary social-scientific study of the New Testament) I had developed in collaboration with others. What would be the defining themes of Second Temple Judaism on the one hand and the first two centuries of Christianity on the other? (This study forms the bulk of *The New Testament and the People of God* [1992].) I came to a conclusion that I had not anticipated. The worldviews are very similar. Both are rooted in the creational monotheism of Israel's Scriptures. Both are passionate about the divine faithfulness to the covenant. Both have a measure of joy, and a measure of hope. But the proportions are radically different. For the Second Temple Jews, the dominant note, as I have just said, was hope, albeit backed up by the joyful ancient stories of divine faithfulness. For the early Christians, however, the dominant note was clearly joy, albeit still including an ongoing hope. The reasons for this joy, and its character, remain recognizably within the ancient Israelite parameters (the celebrations of Exodus, and so forth). But the older picture has been brought into new, sharp, and startling focus by the events concerning Jesus. Whatever explanation one might give of these events —if, for instance, a skeptic were to say that the whole thing was a fabrication based on wish fulfillment—one still has to give a historical account of what the early Christians themselves would have said, and indeed did say, about the reasons for and the shape of this joy.

The usual word studies have been done many times, focusing particularly on the roots *agalliasis* and *chara/chairō* and their cognates. These are frequently combined (e.g., Matt. 5:12; Luke 1:14; 1 Pet. 1:8; 4:13; Rev. 19:7). They occur across the whole range of the New Testament, from the angelic joy (to be shared with "all people") at the birth of Jesus (Luke 2:10-11) through to the joy when the final kingdom is revealed (Rev. 19:6-7). (It is sometimes claimed that there is theological significance in the etymological proximity between *chara*, "joy," and *charis*, "gift." There may be a grain of truth in this, but since the New Testament writers do not seem to me to make this link explicit we should be wary of going beyond the usual rule: the meaning of a word is its use in context, not its history or family resemblances.)

In the Gospels, references to "joy" frequently describe the reaction of crowds or individuals at meeting Jesus or experiencing his healing power. But this goes beyond the natural human gladness at healing and hope. There is both a *theological* and an *eschatological* dimension to this joy. This comes out most clearly in Luke 15, where Jesus describes "joy in heaven" when a sinner repents—in order to explain why he himself is having a celebration with "sinners." The point is made explicitly in the first two parables of the collection, the "lost sheep" and the "lost coin" (Luke 15:1-10). Then, by strong implication within the narrative itself, the same point is to be understood within the third story, the so-called prodigal son or prodigal father (Luke 15:11-32). Here the verb used is *euphrainô* (four times from vv. 23-32), though the parallel with 15:7, 10 indicates that the meaning is to be understood as close to *chara* there.

The emphasis throughout the chapter is on the *appropriateness* of celebration, of "joy," *as a result of what has happened and is happening* in the welcome of (repentant) "sinners"—in other words, as a result of what is happening in the public career of Jesus. And, by implication, as a result of what will happen at its conclusion: "This son of mine," and then "this brother of yours" "was dead and has come to life" (15:24, 32). The public career of Jesus, characterized by (among other things) his celebrations with "sinners," will reach its appropriate climax in his death and resurrection, and the whole thing together explains why celebration, "joy"—in the form of feasting, music, and dancing (15:25)—is not only appropriate in itself but constitutes a sharing of the joy of heaven, that is, of God himself. This is a moment when heaven and earth come together, as in the temple. And this theological dimension is matched by the eschatological: the story of the son who is lost and found, dead and alive again, reflects the dominant Jewish story of the period, that of shameful exile and rapturous return. It is the story Jesus' contemporaries were eager to experience in full at last. It is the story that, in one way and another, Jesus was telling and enacting wherever he went.

The "joy" we see in the Gospels is thus not simply the natural human delight in times of healing and reconciliation, though it is that as well. It is the fresh instantiation, in a new (messianic) mode, of the joy expressed in Psalm 126 and elsewhere: the joy of discovering that Israel's God was at last doing the thing he had promised, rescuing the people from their "exile" and providing forgiveness, restoration, and new life. And it is the joy to be experienced in the fresh *presence* of

God—not now, after all, in a rebuilt temple, but in the person and the actions of Jesus—and also the fresh *act* of God, rescuing people not now from Egypt or Babylon but from death itself.

John's Gospel extends this perspective, and particularly in the Farewell Discourses of chapters 13–17 speaks repeatedly both of Jesus' own joy and of the disciples' sharing in that joy (e.g. 14:28; 15:11; 16:20-24; 17:13). This is despite the repeated warnings of suffering to come, of opposition and persecution from "the world": the world will rejoice at Jesus' demise, but this will be overturned in the events that follow. The context in John indicates that this, too, is not simply the natural human delight at ill fortune suddenly reversed. The whole Gospel is about the new creation that comes about through the "tabernacling" presence of the Word of God (1:14): in other words, the new temple, from which living water will flow out, as in Ezekiel (John 7:37-39). As with Luke, the reader is meant to detect the theological reason for joy (the presence, and rescuing action, of Israel's God) and the eschatological reason (here, the "new temple").

The four Gospels thus link their narrative, and with it their theme of joy, to the ancient hope of Israel, to the biblical promises and prospects that, so they claim, are now finding a new and different kind of fulfillment. But the difference between, say, what a Second Temple Jew might be hoping for and what a reader of the Gospels might be discovering does not consist in the usually imagined distinction between an "earthly" hope on the one hand and a "spiritual" hope on the other. Far from it. The reason for the new "joy" is that certain things are happening "on earth as in heaven." The character of the new "joy," like that of the old, is feasting, a celebration of the goodness of the present creation.

In the letters of Paul, "joy" takes second place only to "love," *agapē*. The fact that these, and seven others, are part of "the fruit of the Spirit" (Gal. 5:22-23) does not mean they somehow grow

49

spontaneously without moral or spiritual effort. They are virtues, to be practiced. But they are not, of course, self-generated. For Paul, the spirit creates the conditions for the new human characteristics to come to birth. Once again these conditions have to do with the fulfillment of the ancient expectation of Israel, the fulfillment also of the Second Temple Jewish hope—though not in the form that had been imagined.

In particular, for Paul "joy" is intimately connected to the resurrection of Jesus on the one hand and to his ascended lordship on the other. This goes wider than mere word studies. The words for "joy" or "rejoicing" do not occur in Romans 8, but one can hardly read that passage without a sense that what is being expressed is joy of the highest quality. There as elsewhere Paul is drawing on the ancient Exodus narrative, seeing it as newly accomplished in the events concerning Jesus. (Romans 6: the slaves come through the water to freedom; Romans 7: arriving at Sinai and the problem of Torah's condemnation; Romans 8: journeying to the "inheritance.") Romans 8 is thus Paul's own fresh equivalent of the song of Miriam, looking at the defeated forces of sin and death and celebrating the divine victory, the revelation of divine covenant faithfulness. Similar things could be said of the "apocalyptic" passage in 1 Cor. 15:20-28, in which Paul draws on Psalms 2, 8, and 110 to claim that Jesus is *already* reigning as Messiah, that he is in the process of completing his victory over all enemies, and that when death itself is finally conquered then this messianic kingdom will give way to the ultimate and final "kingdom of God." This same theme is closely cognate with the passages about Jesus' victorious lordship in Phil. 2:6-11 and 3:20-21. This takes us to the letter that is generally acknowledged as the most explicit Pauline statement of "joy."

Philippians is both an expression of joy and an invitation to joy. This is not because the circumstances, either of Paul himself or of the

Philippian church, are comfortable. He is in prison; they are suffering for the gospel. But joy abounds in all directions. Paul prays with joy (1:4). He rejoices in his present imprisonment (1:18). He longs for their progress and joy in the faith (1:25). Their loving unity will make his joy complete (2:2). He rejoices with them and wants them to rejoice with him (2:17, 18). The return of Epaphroditus will bring them joy, so they must receive him with joy (2:28, 29). The central command of the second half of the letter is simply that they should rejoice (3:1; 4:4); the second of these passages, uniquely in Paul, involves a repetition ("Again I will say, Rejoice"). The Philippians themselves are his "joy and crown" (4:1), an accolade also awarded to the Thessalonians (1 Thess. 2:19-20). Paul himself is rejoicing that they have been able to send him practical help (Phil. 4.10). And these verbal occurrences are simply the tip of the iceberg, signs of the larger theme of the letter as a whole. Philippians is itself a celebration, a sustained declaration of joy in God, joy in the gospel, joy in the Lord, joy despite adverse circumstances, joy expressed in faith and hope and love and, above all, unity.

Again, we enquire as to the reason for, and the character of, this joy. Why was Paul so particularly joyful in writing this letter? And what exactly did he mean by "rejoice" or "celebrate"?

At one level the answer is obvious. Paul and the Philippians clearly had a deep bond of mutual affection. What's more, as the parallel reference in 1 Thessalonians indicates, Paul regarded the churches of northern Greece with particular delight. They were the proof, the seal, the sign that he really was the apostle to the gentiles, that his work was "not in vain." (Why he saw them thus, with the churches of Turkey already established and the church in Corinth yet to come, is another matter.) But there seems to be something more. I believe it is no coincidence that Philippians, as well as being the most explicit letter when it comes to joy, is also the most explicit when it comes to the sovereign lordship of Jesus, and the way in which allegiance to him works out in the wider social and political landscape. This is not the time for a full exploration of these themes, which, like "joy" itself, permeates much of the letter. But we may at least say this.

The central poem about Jesus in Phil. 2:6-11, now widely recognized to be the theological heart of the letter, has many biblical and theological resonances, but at its center it is a celebration of *the radically different kind of lordship* attained, and now exercised, by Jesus. It picks up the larger themes of Isaiah 40–55, in which Israel's God triumphs over the pagan gods and lords of Babylon and reveals his royal presence in the strangest of ways, through the work of the "servant" (Isa. 52:7-12 with 52:13—53:12; Isa. 45:23 is quoted explicitly at Phil. 2:10). The joy that suffuses the whole central section of Isaiah is based on this victorious divine sovereignty, revealed in this way, and Paul encapsulates the same quality through his reworking of these themes with Jesus at their heart.

The specific target is, it seems to me, quite obvious (though this remains controversial and has to be stated with care): *Jesus is Lord, and Caesar is not.* Caesar offers a "salvation," of sorts; the followers of Jesus have their own kind of "salvation," and must work out, with fear and trembling, what this will mean in practice (2:12-13). "Fear and trembling," in the Bible, are the normal reactions to the divine presence, and Paul makes this explicit (2:13). The Jesus believers in Philippi lived in a Roman colony where the power and divinity of Rome and the imperial family were all too present and obvious. Paul wants it to be obvious to them that the power and divinity of the One God celebrated by Isaiah—and now revealed in the crucified Jesus!—are also present, and that the "salvation" they provide is the larger and greater reality. This is the source of, and the reason for, the joy on which he insists.

Paul's own example provides a microcosmic vision of the same thing. He is in prison, quite possibly facing death. And the very fact of his being there has meant that the whole imperial guard have come to hear the "gospel," the royal announcement of Jesus as the crucified and risen lord of the world (1:12-14). The sovereign lordship of the Messiah frames, and renders joyful, his reflections on his likely fate (1:18-26). Then, in offering himself as the model of abandoning privileges in order to "be found in him" (3:9), Paul expresses his joy at "the righteousness from God based on faith," further defined as "to know Christ and the power of his resurrection and the sharing of his sufferings" (3:10). This is not simply about personal fulfillment and hope. "The power of his resurrection" points ahead once more—this is where the strands of the whole letter come together—to Phil. 3:20-21, where Paul declares that "Lord Jesus Messiah" has the *power* to subject all things to himself, and that he will exercise this power in coming from heaven to transform the present world, and with it the bodies of his people. Unlike those in Philippi (perhaps including some of the Christians) whose citizenship is in Rome, the true citizenship of Jesus' followers is in heaven. This does not mean that Paul is here talking about their "going to heaven" one day, any more than the Roman citizens in Philippi would expect to go to live in Rome one day (as people sometimes mistakenly suppose). Rather, they are part of the extended empire of "heaven." The reason why Rome established colonies was partly because central Italy was far too small for all the original military veterans and their families, and partly because Rome was eager to "Romanize" the major locations of the empire. Jesus' people in Philippi are thus a "colony of heaven," responsible for bringing heaven's rule to bear in their own sphere. The lord of heaven, on his return, will make their status complete by transforming their bodies to be like his own (compare 1 Cor. 15:51-54). (We note that the New Testament never uses the word *heaven* for "the place where God's people go when they die." Paul can speak about this intermediate state, after bodily death and before bodily resurrection, but he never calls it "heaven"; here in Philippians [e.g. 1:23], it simply means being "with the Messiah," which is far better.)

This, I propose, indicates the source of, and the reason for, the "joy" of which Paul speaks. It is not simply a spiritual exhilaration, though clearly for Paul it includes that. It is certainly not a sense that though the present world is in bad shape the followers of Jesus will one day leave it behind and go to a better place entirely. Paul has nothing in common with the joy, such as it is, of the gnostic. No: the source of Paul's joy is that the resurrection and enthronement of Jesus, his "lordship" over the world, has created a new world, and with it a new worldview. The followers of Jesus understand that the rule of Caesar, and all other pagan powers, is a mere sham, a parody of the truth, and that the truth now revealed in Jesus is the truth glimpsed and celebrated in Isaiah and the Psalms (Paul refers, here as elsewhere, to Psalms 8 and 110). The Creator God has announced the verdict; the world has been put right; the trees in the field will clap their hands. A new world has been launched, even in the midst of the present old, corrupt, and decaying world. Those who follow Jesus, who are "found in the Messiah," are already part of it. That is why Paul rejoices, and why he summons the Philippians to rejoice with him. And their joy must express itself in the *unity* of the church as a publicly known fact (1:27—2:4, coupled with 2:12-18).

It would be possible to trace the resonances of this theme through the other Pauline letters. There, as in Philippians, we notice that the usual early Christian "now and not yet" obtains just as much: "Not that I have already obtained this or have already reached the goal," as he says in Phil. 3:12. But—and this is vitally important—the present "not yet," including suffering, imprisonment, and death, is not simply something to be pushed to one side as irrelevant. It too is actually part of the *reason for* the "joy" of which Paul speaks.

This answers to the famous passage in Rom. 5:1-5, where, though the verb *kauchaomai* does not really mean "rejoice," as in many English translations, the effect is much the same. "We boast in our hope of sharing the glory of God," declares Paul, and then immediately adds "we also boast in our sufferings, knowing that suffering produces endurance, and endurance produces character, and character produces hope." As in Phil. 3:11, so in Rom. 8:17-30, which leads to the greatest outburst of joy anywhere in the New Testament (8:31-39), the suffering is part of the hope and hence part of the reason for joy. The suffering of the present time is an indication that the new world and the old are chafing together, and that the followers of Jesus are caught between the two. Paul transposes this into the cosmic context in Rom. 8:18-25, interpreting the groaning of all creation as the birth pangs of the new age. This results not in joy *despite* suffering, but in joy *because of* suffering—not in some masochistic sense (Paul is still quite capable of speaking with horror of the pain and anguish he himself has endured, as in 2 Corinthians), but because Paul insists on seeing the suffering in terms of the crucifixion, resurrection, and ascended lordship of Jesus.

With this, we have arrived at an answer to the question with which we began. The disciples returned to Jerusalem after the ascension full of joy because—so the New Testament writers indicate in one way or another—they believed not only that Jesus had been raised from the dead, launching God's new creation, but that he was now enthroned as the world's rightful sovereign. "Heaven," where the ascended Jesus now resides and reigns, is not (as in the implicit Epicureanism of so much modern culture!) a long way away from "earth." The two spheres of the good creation are designed to overlap, to interlock, and eventually to be brought together in perfect harmony forever in the Messiah (Eph. 1:10). This has now happened proleptically in the person of Jesus himself.

Thus, even though other powers and dominions would still do cruel and terrible things, the divine verdict longed for in the ancient Scriptures had been heard, and would be decisive. God had vindicated Jesus after his crucifixion; at his name every knee would bow; and therefore his followers were to "rejoice in the Lord always." In terms of theology and ethics, the virtue of "joy" is inculcated and practiced by the celebration of Jesus as the world's true Lord, who has revealed the true manner of "lordship" in his shameful death, and has thus revealed also the way in which that lordship is presently exercised (that is, through the humble, mourning, peace-making, justice-seeking character sketched in the Beatitudes). In terms of the history of religions, this vision of "joy" comes straight from Israel's Scriptures, with their vision of the triumph of Israel's God over Pharaoh, over Babylon, over all that corrupts and destroys creation. It is the moment of judgment and rescue spoken of again and again by the Psalms and the prophets. And it confronts the vision of pagan celebration that Paul's readers knew only too well from the daily life of their towns and cities.

This leads to the second question. If this is the reason for joy, the source of joy, what is the content of that joy? It has been all too easy in the modern Western world to suppose that *chara* and its cognates refer simply to internal mental or emotional states. Certainly those are involved. It would be farcical to imagine a Christian "joy" that was purely outward show. But I think that in Philippians at least Paul envisages a "celebration" that would involve some kind of *activity*. Granted the traditions Paul inherited, and his solidly physical understanding of the new creation, including the resurrection body, it is inconceivable that he would have thought of celebrating Jesus' lordship with a purely mental or emotional happiness, a purely inward sense of well-being. Paul was no hedonist, but as a robust creational monotheist he believed that "the earth is the Lord's and all that is in it" (Ps. 24:1, quoted in 1 Cor. 10:26), and that food and drink were good and to be enjoyed. Part of the reason for Paul's anxiety about shared table fellowship, and shared worship, in Galatians 2 and Romans 14 and 15, was that Christian meals, not least but not only the Eucharist, constituted a central part of what he meant by *celebrate, rejoice*. The word *celebration* has become almost a technical term, certainly in my own church and perhaps elsewhere, for "holding a Eucharist." We must guard against that becoming a dead metaphor.

But I wonder—this is impossible to prove, but I wonder—whether Paul also envisaged something more. The "celebrations" of *Kyrios Caesar* took place in public, as whole towns would be given over to days and seasons of festivals involving processions, music and dancing, feasting and drinking, and ultimately sacrifices and prayers at the relevant shrines. Most ancient religions did that kind of thing. Did Paul want to encourage the Christians to do their own public "rejoicing," perhaps even as a kind of protest? Was their celebration to be only behind closed doors? As I read Phil. 1:27-30 and 4:4-5, I detect at least the possibility that Paul expected the Christians to be known, *in public*, as people who were celebrating the cosmic lordship of Jesus—with a different kind of celebration, to be sure, in which all people would know their *epieikes*, which perhaps means "restraint" in contrast to the wild excesses of pagan celebrations. I have argued in chapter 13 of *Paul and the Faithfulness of God* that in many senses, despite Protestant fears, Paul's communities did have something that could be called a "religion"—remembering that in the ancient world "religion" was something that whole communities *did* as part of their self-definition. A "religion" in the ancient world, after all, was something that bound together and strengthened the *polis*, the local civic community, through the worship of the local gods. For Paul, there were communal and personal activities that bound together the community of Jesus followers in worship, united with one another and with the Creator God who had made himself known afresh, and decisively, through the gospel. And my suggestion—or at least my question—is whether perhaps "joy," *chara*, in Philippians and elsewhere, might include this outward, and perhaps public, expression of "eschatological religion."

There is no space to pursue the issues raised by "joy" in other New Testament documents. I note simply a few highlights. The Johannine correspondence speaks of the joy that comes from the mutual relationship of writer and readers (1 John 1:4; 2 John 4, 10, 11, 12). First Peter expresses, even more strongly than Paul, the exuberant and unrestrained celebration of joy at believing in the Jesus whose own sufferings have paved the way for those of his followers, transforming them from meaningless agony into the testing of faith and so into the glorious hope (1 Pet. 1:6-9). This corresponds, of course, to scenes in Acts and elsewhere, where persecution is hailed and celebrated as a sign that the believers really are the Messiah's people, really are on the right track (Acts 5:41).

Conclusions

I have concentrated on one or two passages rather than attempting to give a full New Testament picture. As I have hinted, and as is the case with many other themes, a *topic* may be present even when the two or three key *words* are not; but I have here focused on passages in which "joy" is an explicit theme. My basic argument has been that the puzzles we might notice—why do the disciples rejoice when Jesus is taken from them? How can they speak of "joy" when so much is still so wrong with their lives, with the world and its wicked rulers, and so on?—can find answers when we consider how the whole early Christian worldview actually functions. In the place of the dominant note of "hope" that we find in Second Temple Judaism, rooted as that was in creational and covenantal monotheism when facing the horrors and perplexities of life under the Romans, we find the dominant note of "joy," from within the same basic Jewish worldview, and rooted in the same Scriptures, but brought into a startling new focus because of Jesus. I have suggested that in the key passages we see the early Christian belief that in Jesus there had come about a new union between heaven and earth, with the celebrations of the one spilling over necessarily into the celebrations of the other. I have pointed out that "celebrations," within creational monotheism, would naturally involve food and drink, music and dancing, and the other accoutrements of "joy" as expressed outwardly and publicly. (It was after all the public nature of Jesus' celebrations that caused the angry questions to which Luke 15 was the answer.) And I have suggested that both in the Gospels and in the epistles we can trace a link between the sovereignty, the "lordship," of Jesus and the exhortation to, or expression of, "joy." The *fact* of the resurrection and exaltation of the crucified Jesus opens up a new world, launches the new creation, over which Jesus himself is sovereign; that is the root cause of joy. The *manner* of his coming to that sovereignty—his suffering and shameful death—indicates that when we say "Jesus is Lord, and Caesar is not," we are not (as some anxiously suppose) replacing one oppressive or totalizing system with another. Rather, "lordship" itself is transformed into the picture we see in the Beatitudes, or in Mark 10:35-45, or of course supremely in Phil. 2:1-18. In other words—and in terms of our earlier discussion of scriptural antecedents—*something has happened* in which the divine judgment on evil, and the divine rescue of the world from its grip, has been unveiled. This is the new Exodus, the new "return from exile." Yes, the "second coming" is still to take place. But modern exegesis, reflecting a reticence or outright denial concerning the bodily resurrection and ascension, has put far too much weight instead on the early Christian hope for the "parousia" as the reason for joy. Jesus' first followers did indeed celebrate what was still to come. But they did so because of the physical, creation-renewing events that had already taken place.

Where does this leave contemporary discussion of "joy"? As with many themes in early Christian thought and life, we see both significant continuities and significant discontinuities. Joy and celebration, within a creational and new creational monotheism, involve not some superspiritual otherworldly pleasure but the elements of creation itself caught up in new expressions of new creation. This is the birth of sacramental theology within Christianity. Precisely because the early Christians believed, with a faith rooted in Israel's Scriptures, that in Jesus they had discerned the human face of Israel's God, the world's Creator, their celebrations were bound to express significant continuity both with any and all human celebrations and with the Jewish festivals in particular. Hence the way in which Christian baptism celebrates a new kind of Exodus, and the Eucharist a new kind of Passover.

But at the same time there are radical discontinuities. The Jewish celebrations of the Second Temple period, though rooted in the joy of Exodus 15 and the rest, look on to the future with increasing, and ultimately disappointed, urgency. The disasters of 70 and 135 changed the Jewish world forever. Joy remains within Jewish festivals and Torah study, but it may appear to be shorn of its historical and political elements.

Equally, the pagan celebrations of cult and empire were rooted in a different worldview, a different sort of power, and resulted in a different kind of "joy." That is a study worth undertaking in itself.

The early Christian celebrations were a reaffirmation of an essentially Jewish vision of the world, over against that pagan vision. They were not an optional extra for the communities generated by the gospel. Not to celebrate, not to express joy in the lordship of the crucified and risen Jesus, would be tacitly to acknowledge that one did not really believe. The human joy of food and drink, of family and civic life, were taken up and transformed, with many paradoxes along the way, into the Jesus-believing joy of Eucharist and united fellowship. The deep Jewish roots of early Christian joy enable the church's celebrations to confront the world dominated by Caesar with the news of a different empire, a different *kind* of empire. Like love, peace, and the other aspects of the Spirit's fruit, joy may be difficult to maintain. But for the early Christians, nothing could take it away. It was, after all, Jesus' own gift to his people, on the night he was betrayed (John 16:20). The many betrayals that Jesus' followers will then face, both personal and political, global and cosmic, cannot ultimately destroy, but will only further contextualize, that joy.

4

Toward a Theology of Joy

Charles Mathewes

Christians regularly confess that humanity's "chief and highest end is to glorify God, and fully to enjoy him forever," as the Westminster Catechism puts it. But what exactly it is to glorify God, and to enjoy God forever, is a matter of some dispute. In fact, none of us can safely say that we fully understand what those words mean. We are called to a destiny that we can name, but one whose inner energies remain veiled to our eyes, in this dispensation at least.

Nonetheless, though the ultimate meaning of the word *"joy"* remains beyond us, it may offer one useful way to talk about the eschatological destiny of humanity, the vocation and meaning of the churches, and Christian theology as a practice of, in, and for those churches. After all, it is the mission of the churches to enable humanity, in unity with God and community with one another, to fulfill their destiny. And if we understand theology as an attempt to help the churches in their mission, it may be a wise strategic choice to imagine a theological program centered around an ecclesially disciplined cultivation of joy. That, at least, is the thought I will pursue here.

Hence here I want to explore something of what that strategy might entail. Part 1 sketches what I mean by "*joy*," what it means to say that the churches are called to cultivate such joy, and what a "theology of joy" might entail. Part 2 suggests how such a focus on joy might refigure what we can call the "horizon of problematics" that any theology entails—that is, that spectrum of concerns in relation to which a theology is always partly determined, and toward which it attempts in part and more or less self-consciously to speak—in ways that are superior to the rival options for such a "horizon of problematics" on offer today. Finally, part 3 explores the prospects of a broad "alliance for joy," looking for friends in the culture with whom Christians, individually and in their communities, can make various sorts of common cause in the struggle to cultivate joy. This part tries to identify some potential allies, of other professed faiths and of none, and it also suggests some limits to those alliances due to what I judge to be the differences between what Christians mean (or should mean) by "*joy*" and what non-Christians take joy, or its likenesses, to be.

Setting the Stage

I begin by attempting first to sketch, provisionally, what I take "*joy*" to designate, and then, second, to sketch one way to understand the churches' mission, and theological task, as one of cultivating joy in the people of God.

The Nature of Joy

On my account, ecstatic, joyful praise is humanity's end and current glory.[1] The joyful act of praising God—a thankfulness flowing almost automatically from recognition of God's gifts—is the central action of the human, the self-transcending act in which we begin to participate in our fullest flourishing. A larger Augustinian anthropology is implied here, and not an apophatic one: we were never designed simply for human sociability, and attempts to reduce us to that mutilate our natural being, both eschatologically—as creatures called to become fit to bear the joy that is our eschatological destiny—and currently—as we are called to receive rightly the proleptic gifts of that eschatological joy in the here and now. We are always doxological creatures, called to recognize and exult in the vast gratuitous contingency of creation itself, most immediately and locally in how that gratuitous contingency is manifest in our own lives, but ineluctably spilling over into a more proper, and properly cosmic, gratitude to being in general; and that gratitude is itself the ultimate telos of joy. We are called to become participants in the endless joyful round of love that is the Trinity, and though in this dispensation that round has been splintered into a fugal structure, it has not been severed from that end; and so our lives here are a matter of learning to receive rightly the proleptic gifts of eschatological joy today.

What can we say, here and now, about joy? Most fundamentally we can say that joy is excess, beyond conception or imagining; as St. Paul says, quoting Isaiah, "What no eye has seen, nor ear heard, nor the human heart conceived, what God has prepared for those who love him" (1 Cor. 2:9, see Isa. 64:4). Furthermore, this excess is self-referentially recognized *as* excess, and so in awareness of joy

---

1. I have been much informed by a number of works, perhaps especially David F. Ford and Daniel W. Hardy, *Living in Praise: Worshipping and Knowing God*, rev. ed. (Grand Rapids: Baker, 2005), and Hugo Rahner, *Man at Play* (New York: Herder & Herder, 1967).

we are aware of ourselves *as* joyful, but unable fully to comprehend the joy. Unlike happiness—where very little self-consciousness can work to undo the state—joy seems more durable to human reflexivity—indeed, perhaps partially constituted by it. It seems part of the logic of joy that one knows one is joyful (even if that knowledge is hardly a primary fact about one's joy) and that that reflexivity if anything amplifies our joy.

Yet joy is not solipsistic. Certainly the potential self-consciousness of joy is part of why joy can seem at times disorienting, dizzying, revealing an infinite height, or a bottomlessness, intrinsic to joy. But this dizzying is not a wallowing in the infinite sublimity of our own subjectivity. Joy is *provoked* by something contingent, something that comes to one, something outside oneself—the hug of your child, a Thelonious Monk performance of "Crepuscule with Nellie," or the recognition that the cosmos is utterly unique and so warrants an infinite awe and gratitude to the one who brought it into being. Joy seems less a general mood and more a responsive state prompted by some discrete object or action. Joy is a responsive act of exaltation and thankfulness, implicating one in an extrasubjective relationship. In contrast to the (necessarily unself-conscious) immanence of happiness, joy speaks immediately of transcendence, of what is outside.[2]

So joy is excess, and an excess beyond the self. This leads to the second thing to say about joy, which is that, because it is so supremely intimate to oneself yet also intimately related to an other, joy is a reality best understood in the "middle voice"—that is, a reality that is not purely passive, happening to us, nor simply active, something we do; but partaking of both receptivity and dynamism. Other, equally

---

2. I am grateful especially to Marianne Meye Thompson for her essay "Reflections on Joy in the Bible" on these points, though she should of course not be held responsible for what I do with those points here.

significant phenomena in Christian life are also framed in the middle voice; the Koine word for feeling compassion is *splagchnizomai*, which is another crucial "action" that is in the middle voice; and a similar thing can be said of *elthon* ("to arrive" or "to come,") which is used for the prodigal son's recognition, amid the swine, of the reality to which his life has come (of longing for the quality of life of pigs).[3] Hence human agency may be implicated in the achievement of joy in a slightly less indirect way than it can be in the attainment of happiness, which may be why St. Paul repeatedly exhorts people to be joyful (not happy)—for example, Phil. 4:4, "Rejoice in the Lord always; again I will say, rejoice."[4]

Thus understood as an excessive rapture, catching us up into a reality in the "middle voice," joy is a sort of sacramental state: *in* creation yet prompted ultimately by something beyond and before creation, a reality simultaneously speaking of immediacy and transcendence, something done *to* you yet something you manifest, express, realize, and participate in. Here and there, now and not yet, you and another, creation and Creator—joy can serve as a synecdoche of the Christian life as a whole. And that is how I propose to understand it here.

The Role of the Churches and Theology in Cultivating Joy

Joy so understood is one conceptual lens through which we can understand the struggle to lead a Christian life. As such, this struggle is, or ought to be, an ecclesial struggle, before and as it is an individual

---

3. *Splagchnizomai*—to "feel compassion" (Luke 15:20 and elsewhere)—eight of the twelve uses in the NT refer to Jesus feeling compassion for others (Matt. 9:36; 14:14; 15:32; 18:27 (*not Jesus*); 20:34; Mark 1:41; 6:34; 8:2;, 9:22 (*not Jesus, but compassion asked of him by another*); Luke 7:13; 10:33 (*not Jesus, the Samaritan*); 15:20 (*not Jesus, but father of the Prodigal*)). *Elthon*—"came to himself" (Luke 15:17). I thank Rebekah Latour for help with this matter.
4. Jean-Luc Marion's *The Erotic Phenomenon*, trans. Stephen E. Lewis (Chicago: The University of Chicago Press, 2006) is useful in thinking about agency here.

one. That is, for theological, ethical, and sociological reasons, a theology of joy must be a church theology.

This implies a fairly specific understanding of what a church is, and it is this: the churches are those institutions that aim to give us a communal and personal, intellectual and affective, structure to help cultivate joy, our cultivation of which is their ultimate purpose. They shape a liturgically structured discipline whereby we are "trained by our longings" to become fit citizens of the kingdom of heaven.[5] Indeed, the churches just are the way that sinful humanity is made into the body of Christ and comes to participate in the divine self-giving that is the Trinity. They are those communities where the grace of Christ, and the joy that flows from it, is most intentionally and intensively *solicited*, its reception *cultivated*, and through that cultivation most palpably and vividly *endured*. It is solicited, cultivated, and endured, in two ways: first, through the primary practice (most commonly begun in worship services in church, but hopefully over time extending throughout our lives) of showing us how the story of our lives are only properly intelligible within God's providential governance and God's saving action upon the world; and second, by the derivative communal response to those stories, the actions that those stories can narrate and for which they provide determinate structure, showing us thereby how that story carries on, with us in it, to its joyful consummation. This response is directed to God both immediately—in prayer, praise, and thanksgiving—and in and through the mediation of sacramental acts of justice, charity, and peacemaking in the world, through the world, to God. In all

---

5. Augustine, *Homilies on 1 John* 4.6, in *Augustine: Later Works*, ed. John Burnaby (Philadelphia: Westminster, 1955), 290. See Carol Harrison, *Augustine: Christian Truth and Fractured Humanity* (New York: Oxford University Press, 2000), 97. The idea of "beginning" as a goal to be sought was a central trope in early monastic spirituality; see Douglas Burton-Christie, *The Word in the Desert: Scripture and the Quest for Holiness in Early Christian Monasticism* (New York: Oxford University Press, 1993), 247–49 (though the book as a whole has been of enormous value for me).

this activity, humans are trained for the eschatological reception of creation *as* creation, to undertake the light burden of the yoke of Christ and undergo the training that is necessary for humans to become fit to bear the weight of glory that is humankind's eschatological destiny—to begin the arduous but joyful journey to becoming those who understand and inhabit what it means to be part of a created order loved into existence by God—whose love is not simply *admiration*, akin to a warm beam of admiration from a distant sun, but *constitution*, like the hot blood that surges through our flesh, and the very flesh itself. "The church" is the activity of the people of God as the body of Christ being trained to bear the Holy Spirit in its practice of being the love of the Father for the Son and the love of the Son for the Father. This is not a training that humans inaugurate, of course; we discover ourselves always already on the way in this training, and on some level the most we do is beseech the Spirit to come. The churches are simply the location where that training has its central locus in human history.

It is only as such—as first and foremost a *church* theology—that this proposal is a political theology. Hence, I suspect, only by coming clear on the central pedagogical and ascetical tasks of the Christian churches, and the central ecclesio-centric focus of theology, can theology say something of real, if immediately indirect, import to this-worldly political order. The maladies of the soul that the churches diagnose are not unrelated to the maladies of the polity that much political discourse currently laments, and will, as I have argued, increasingly in the future bewail; and the pedagogy that the churches undertake is effective, primarily indirectly, for those more immediately political concerns as well. The churches can make good citizens, then, and a theology can be political, most basically by teaching believers what it really means when they pray, *veni creator spiritus.*

This could sound like I am recommending that we understand the churches as a spiritual gymnasium. I do not mean that, however, and this is where theology as a distinctive discourse and intellectual practice plays a role. For theology, on this account, provides an intellectual framework within which to understand the practices and preaching of the churches as a form of theopolitical soul crafting and community creation whose ultimate purpose is to enable for its members an embodied deliberative life that cultivates a hopeful joy. And as joy is in the middle voice, so this intellectual framework highlights for us how such soul crafting is not something we primarily do, but that is done *to* us—how our stories are always already caught up in the sacramental dialectic of the already and not yet, helping us see how the proleptic *already* is palpable amid the *not yet* all-too-obvious in our quotidian, sin-riddled world.

Theology then has as its topic of study how humans are taken up, in and through praise, into vivifying communion with God even now—the ultimate goal of all theology is of course evangelical: to help Christian communities pursue the deepening (in its members' souls, through various broadly "ascetical" practices) and widening (in others, and society as a whole) of the body of Christ on earth, the church. *Lex orandi, lex credendi*: "The law of prayer is the law of belief." This is one of the oldest of Christian theological rules; it means that proper theological formulations, of what it is right to believe, always attend seriously to how people want to pray. The voice of the people as they pray to God in thanks and praise—however that "voice" is to be determined (and that is a hard task indeed)—is an ineliminable criterion of theological propriety. And behind the people, guiding them, is the Holy Spirit. Theology is an attempt to understand the Holy Spirit—to catch its rhythm, so to speak; it is a way of dancing, where another takes the lead. It is a way of making sense of our active gratitude, expressed in "prayer" that, when most broadly construed, includes our works as well as our words. Because of this, such theology holds itself accountable in a certain way to the Christian community's (often but not always previously) considered theological views. In short, theology consists finally of recommendations to the faithful, finally about how they can increase their ability to praise—that is, how best to increase their ability to participate in the life of praise that always already constitutes the flourishing of the body of Christ, the churches' liturgy of citizenship that fits us for the celestial republic.

This does not mean that a theology centered around the cultivation of joy is ruthlessly pragmatically tied to immediate demands for church relevance. It is not simply a rather low to the ground therapeutic ethics, helping us to see what it is to live and be happy only in the *distentio* that is hope. It is also properly a metaphysics, a way of seeing creation as creation, and indeed as yet incomplete, waiting to be fully realized in the eschaton.

Indeed, much of the history of theology can be understood as an attempt to grapple with the fraught relationship between joy and the created order, at once absolutely necessary and utterly opaque. I have already said that it is so in Augustine, but consider Aquinas: In the *responsio* to the first article of the first *quaestio* of the *Summa theologiae*, Aquinas quotes Isa. 64:4 as evidence as to why a *sacra doctrina* that stands beyond (natural?) human reason is required. Joy, it seems for Aquinas, is simultaneously the mysterious "otherworldly" prompting force behind *sacra doctrina* and the ultimate destiny of created human existence, a destiny whose tug is palpable even now. Aquinas is complemented in this by an insistence, more tacit in him than overt, that this joy, though it be obscurely present in our world, is yet still incarnate here, and informing the world; so we can borrow from Augustine and say that the restlessness of our hearts absent their resting in God (in *Confessions* 1.1), which is part of our

71

creation, is itself also a function of joy. So the apparently suprarational reality of joy, of grace, has descended, as it were, into creation, and become incarnate in it, perpetually ensuring the created order does not become too stagnant in dulled indifference to its Creator. Hence, just as joy exists at the junction between transcendence and immanence, now and not yet, so does the practice of theology as well.

Of course the puzzle of how this can be so is simply one part of the logic of Christian faith altogether, a faith that in this life is caught always in the ascetical struggle to keep the polarities described above in an eschatological tension. In this undertaking, believers always struggle to avoid the "fleshly imagination," misconceptions of joy grounded in the criteria and ideals of this fallen dispensation, images that domesticate or (mis-)secularize such joy. And this may be especially a struggle in ages such as ours, where so much of culture, politics, and social life are about our immediate gratification. But in fact, this is also a challenge for all times, and so in this way, the struggle properly to understand, and rightly to cultivate, joy is a perennial struggle for us.

The priority of this talk about joy may seem odd as a description of what theology is, what Christian churches are supposed to cultivate. Christianity has often been seen by modern critics as a force oppressing human joy—a device for making people feel guilty, a way to express some fundamental animus at the world, not a vehicle for delight in it. And H. L. Mencken was not entirely off base when he once defined Puritanism as "the haunting fear that someone, somewhere, may be happy."[6] It is also the case, however, that it has

---

6. Alistair Cooke, ed., *The Vintage Mencken* (New York: Vintage Books, 1955), 233. Mencken was a shallow Nietzschean; but a deeper, and more probing Nietzschean response, from the likes of someone like Foucault, would not disagree with that—it would simply recognize that every social order shapes subjects in powerful ways, including in their emotional and affective lives, and Christianity is no different.

given voice to some of the greatest expressions of joy that humans have so far imagined. And whatever the history of the Puritans would suggest, the history of Christian revival movements—including, in recent decades, the emergence of a vibrantly expressive and joyful form of Christian worship, in the exploding Pentecostal movement across the world—gives evidence of powerful dynamics toward exuberance and delight deeply rooted in the tradition. I want to recognize such non-Christians' suspicions of Christian accounts of joy, and I hope to be heard as partly and indirectly responding to them; but I do not want my proposal to be governed by them, or to be read defensively, as centrally and directly aimed at disputing such accusations. I note them here only to recognize their presence as a factor that any theology of joy must recognize.

Joy and *Metanoia*?

One last thought. There is the question of whether Christians themselves are fully able to stand behind a program centered upon a pedagogy of joy. After all, some reasonably question whether "joy" as a category can ever really capture the full range of *metanoia*, which involves *justice* and *judgment* as well. Perhaps focusing on joy alone would risk undervaluing the ways we should cooperate with God to work for the world's good (*justice*), and perhaps it avoids the difficult work of discerning God's will more directly (*judgment*). That is, we cannot forget that joy is only one dimension of the eschatological aim, and a too-exclusive focus on this word could easily return us to a kind of consumerist mindset.

This is wise and true. "Joy" is at best a noble lie, a human term applied to divine realities, and any such application will be flawed; recall Aquinas's *incept* for theology: this-worldly human knowing will always only be achieved by a few, *et per longum tempus, et cum admixtione multorum errorum homini proveniret.*[7] Yet, if we proceed with due caution and circumspection, I suspect that a theology of joy might well produce new and surprisingly fruitful lines of enquiry.

Some of those lines of enquiry focus on the various, more immediately practical, challenges any such theology organized around joy must face. I turn to them next.

Our Challenge: Joylessness

Thinking about the Christian theological task, and the purpose of the churches, as a matter of preparing humans for the joy that is our eschatological destiny is not only interesting for what it says about the vocation and meaning of the churches and the inner logic of the theological task. It also has the substantial value of helping us better specify and comprehend the true challenges that Christian life faces, perhaps in any age but especially in our conditions today, in late modernity. For there are, as ever, snakes in this particular garden. Our current situation makes it hard, harder than it should be, to cultivate joy; indeed some think that the human capacity for joy is under quite severe and historically unique attack. This section assesses those claims, in order to come to an understanding of the challenges we truly face.

In doing this we are both showing how this theological vision understands the challenges we face today, and we are arguing that this way of understanding those challenges is the best one available. This last point is especially important, because here I think we find rival and in their own ways compelling demonologies of our moment. Most especially we are tempted by two rival languages of theopolitical concern. One sees our fundamental problems through the prism of a classic liberal concern (now extended into some forms

---

7. *Summa Theologiae*, Prima pars, q.1 a.1.

of postmodern concern) with totalitarianism and the oppression of the human spirit; thinkers as diverse as Kant, liberation theologians of various stripes, and various postmodern deconstruction theologies all share this concern. The other, which we can call the aristocratic critique of our democratic-egalitarian age, sees our fundamental problems through the lens of long-standing anxieties about the decay of absolute standards of perfection and true nobility, a decay ending in what thinkers in this vein call "nihilism"; in this group we see a line of critics going from Tocqueville through Nietzsche and Weber to contemporary worriers like Francis Fukuyama and John Milbank.

Now both of these are worthwhile concerns. And I do not mean to discard the positive insights each offers. But I think that neither of them really gets at the full depth and breadth of the challenges we face. Total oppression has been a real and powerful danger for some in the past; but most of us in the West are not most immediately or most fundamentally confronted with totalitarian terror. And it is certainly the case that we have entered a Brave New World where almost any desire can be met, letting us enjoy the quotidian *divertissements* of the last men, at least until death overtakes us. But neither of these horizons of problematics really capture the theo-psychological depth of our problem—at least not as well as an Augustinian political theology of joy and idolatry do.

Lest my imminent grouchiness be mistaken for apocalypticism, I should begin with a frank statement: we have never had it so good. The market world we live in brings us benefits and blessings unimagined by our ancestors. Our material lives are richer by far than any age before us; your typical working-class person in the first world lives amid more material comforts than did nineteenth-century royalty. (It is an astonishing fact that increasingly across the developed world, the central emerging medical problem is obesity.) Across the globe, the last several decades have seen the largest expansion of human wealth in recorded history.[8] There is an interesting, and at least partially plausible, case to be made that the bourgeois virtues cultivated in this world are genuine moral virtues, fitting more and more of us for flourishing and rich lives. And the worries I express in the coming pages should not be taken as an expression fundamentally of regret that the scope for human agency has expanded and continues to expand at breathtaking pace. Far from it: there remain too many people in the world for whom too much agency is hardly a looming danger. None of this can be denied, nor should anyone take seriously complaints about this situation that suggest that it would be better for humanity, on the whole or individually, if we were to go back to the way we lived two or three centuries ago. Certainly individuals are free to "simplify" their lives if they so wish; but it must be noted that even such decisions are just that—free choices, enabled as such by life in our world. (The genuine crisis of the environment that we face is not, I think, an essential part of this world, but epiphenomenal upon it—it can be solved while the fundamental dynamics continue.) And few who talk about going "back to the land" are really able to do so without relying on modern medicine, government, technology, and education. Like it or not, this is our world—and there is a very great deal of *good* in it.

But these facts should not induce in us any Pollyannaish placidity, nor seduce us toward a smug dismissal of those who feel something is missing. Despite the hyperbolic hysteria of (typically well-paid) demonologists of the market, this world poses real dangers for its inhabitants, as its blessings bring with them enormous and complicated challenges. Most fundamentally we face the prospect that the conditions of our existence militate against our inhabiting

8. The World Bank's Development Research Group estimates that from 2005 to 2008, the number of people living at .25/day or $ 2/day declined—both as an absolute number *and* as a percentage of the population, across all regions of the world.

integral, coherent, and deep lives, lives of the sort that humanity has talked about trying to live for most of its time on this earth, and lives of the sort that Christians cultivating joy ought to seek to lead.

Contemporary Challenges: Consumerism, Agency, and the Limits of Choice

Let me try to sketch what I mean by these worries. At least since Daniel Bell's *The Cultural Conditions of Capitalism*, thinkers have worried that the basic structures of liberal capitalist consumerist society strongly encourage the development of a culture of luxury that vitiates the energies its members need to develop into a virtuous citizenry. (If Albert Hirschman is right, these worries go back to basic debates about the passions versus the interests in the eighteenth century.) The details of this worry are complex and contested, but the basic concern is that our cultures embody a soul craft profoundly inimical to proper moral agency. Most basically this happens because the "creative destruction" that is the society's basic energy creates in us a radical existential turbulence that constantly undermines, directly and indirectly, the stability and commitment to long-term aims that has been the fundament of moral formation in traditional societies.

To see what this "radical existential turbulence" amounts to, consider how pervasive dissatisfaction is in consumer societies. In order to prosper, these societies require constant cultivation of dissatisfaction in consumers—the "warranted obsolescence" not only of the products we buy, but of our satisfaction with those products themselves. Such dissatisfaction would be intolerable without some overarching acceptance of such dissatisfaction as, curiously, satisfactory; you need some way to survive a life lived fundamentally in the experience of lack. So this lifestyle entails a therapeutic project of ensuring a minimally positive outlook on life, irrespective of whether such an outlook is warranted by reality. The goal is to feel good, to exist in the subjective feeling of self-worth and accomplishment. But feeling good has no very vital connection to the condition of actually being morally good; hence we aim to be "nice," not good—socially acceptable and civically inoffensive. Such psychological cosmetology need be little more than skin-deep to succeed, and so it is. In the rituals of late-modern selfhood, the problem is not that self-knowledge and moral rectitude are sacrificed on the altar of happiness; it is simply that, in these rituals, such concepts play no functional role at all.[9]

All this radically changes our picture of ourselves and our world. As Iris Murdoch put it, "Man is a creature who makes pictures of himself and then comes to resemble the picture."[10] When we imagine

9. See Colin Campbell, *The Romantic Ethic and the Spirit of Modern Consumerism* (Oxford: Basil Blackwell, 1987), esp. 138–60, and "I Shop Therefore I Know That I Am: The Metaphysical Foundations of Modern Consumerism," in *Elusive Consumption*, ed. Karin Ekstrom and Helen Brembeck (Oxford: Berg, 2004).

   The literature on therapy is vast. Much real Freudian therapy seeks *un*happiness; see Eric Santner, *On the Psychotheology of Everyday Life: Reflections on Freud and Rosenzweig* (Chicago: The University of Chicago Press, 2001); and Jonathan Lear, *Happiness, Death, and the Remainder of Life* (Cambridge, MA: Harvard University Press, 2002). For a very interesting study contrasting "eudaimonic" pictures of human flourishing—that is, pictures of human flourishing that identify flourishing with the exercise of agency along lines conducive to an objectively structured human nature—with "hedonic" pictures—that is, subjective pleasure-based pictures of human flourishing—and arguing that eudaimonic pictures are superior to hedonic ones in tracking the reported evidence of human life satisfaction (even among those who profess a more "hedonic" picture of human happiness), see Ethan A. McMahan and David Estes, "Hedonic versus Eudaimonic Conceptions of Well-Being: Evidence of Differential Associations with Self-Reported Well-Being," *Social Indicators Research* 103 (2011): 93–108. For more, see John P. Robinson, "Sex, Arts, and Verbal Abilities: Three Further Indicators of How American Life Is Not Improving," *Social Indicators Research* 99 (2010): 1–12. See also Robert Lane, *The Loss of Happiness in Market Democracies* (New Haven: Yale University Press, 2001).

10. Iris Murdoch, "Metaphysics and Ethics," in *The Nature of Metaphysics*, ed. D. F. Pears (London: MacMillan, 1960), 121. On the link between studying rational choice economics and selfishness, see Robert H. Frank, Thomas Gilovich, and Dennis T. Regan, "Does Studying Economics Inhibit Cooperation?" *Journal of Economic Perspectives* 7, no. 2 (Spring 1993): 159–71; and Robert H. Frank, Thomas Gilovich, and Dennis T. Regan, "Do Economists Make Bad Citizens?" *Journal of Economic Perspectives* 10, no. 1 (Winter 1996): 187–92. On the link to depressed voting, see André Blais and Robert Young, "Why Do People Vote? An Experiment in Rationality," *Public Choice* 99 (1999): 39–55. For evidence against the selfishness hypothesis, see Bruno S. Frey and Stephan Meier, "Are Political Economists Selfish and Indoctrinated? Evidence from a Natural Experiment," *Economic Inquiry* 41, no. 3 (July

ourselves as fundamentally mobile agents adrift on a bottomless sea of consumable objects, it is not only our conception of action that is distorted; it becomes very difficult to see much point in the idea of a central underlying purpose to life as a whole. Pascal's *divertissement*—a word we might translate (with a Parisian *audace*) from Pascal's French as "the channel-surfing of the soul"[11]—is no longer the temptation of the leisured elite; it becomes the habituated lifestyle of us all.

It is at this moment that liberal worries about the oppression of human agency seem beside the point, and worries about nihilism have their strongest bite. For indeed, in a certain light, we do look like Nietzsche's "Last Men," Weber's "specialists without spirit, sensualists without heart." More recent thinkers have bemoaned this as well—Fukuyama's *End of History* thesis effectively argues this point, and David Brooks's concept of "flexidoxy" and Jonathan Rauch's idea of "apatheism" do something of the same on a more popular level. Within theological circles, the fixation on nihilism is quite common among a certain species of theological voices.

But I think that this is importantly mistaken. For consider: if choice is all there is, and which choice you make makes no difference, yet still the necessity of choice is real. There remains an absolute in this schema, a *summum bonum* higher than which cannot be conceived: namely the good of choice itself. Now this is patently absurd, of course, but it has a sufficient patina of plausibility to make for a superficially coherent life plan. Choice becomes God; it serves, that is, as an idol (an ideologically imagined idol, of course, but in the end what idol isn't that?). The problem that so many have described

<hr />

2003): 448–62. Accepting this fact needn't move you towards any sort of flat-footed idealism, of course; it only helps you avoid flat-footed materialism.

11. On *divertissement*, see Blaise Pascal, *Pensées sur la religion et sur quelques autres sujets*, ed. Louis Lafuma (Paris: Editions de Luxembourg, 1951), § 136. *Pensées*, trans. A. J. Krailsheimer (Baltimore: Penguin Books, 1966), 37–41. And see Alasdair MacIntyre, *After Virtue*, 2nd ed. (Notre Dame: University of Notre Dame Press, 1984), 24ff., for a discussion of the "aesthete" as a modern type.

as nihilism, that is to say, is really a problem of idolatry, and more specifically the pathetic idolatry of bare choice itself. But approaches that focus on concerns about nihilism fail to take this insight organically on, and thereby deprive themselves not only of a powerful diagnostic tool, but also of a more charitable attitude toward our condition.

This critique is important in part for the positive lesson it teaches us about the sorts of creatures that we are revealed, by it, to be. The self-conscious exercise of agency cannot be the ultimate good: would it be good for you to *choose* each breath you take? To *choose* each step? A worldview of absolute choice, however superior it may seem to us when we compare it with what we imagine of previous worldviews, is subtly tyrannical. It misshapes us, so that we come to care less *what* we choose and more *that* we choose. But surely some of the things we "choose" are not really "choices" on our part at all. Most superficially, our hobbies are not simply chosen; there is something about model trains, or baseball, or antique cars, or Celtic folk music, or weaving, or whatever that resonates with you in a more fundamental way than the language of "choice" can capture. Similarly, for those of us who feel our professions as vocations—literally, "callings"—it is not true to our lives to think that we "chose" them. Most profoundly, I cannot speak of "choosing" to love my daughter or my son or my wife without misdescribing the experience I have of being drawn to them, transfixed by them, *just because* of who they are.

The failure of choice to reach deeply into our beings is more damaging still. It is not just a failure of moral rectitude that we witness here. We seem to be witnessing a significant withering of our capacities for joy. Precisely because joy is so profoundly *unchosen*, but is a responsive commitment to what is there before us, demanding of us, it is very difficult indeed to articulate in a worldview so overmastered by the ideology of choice. And that is my complaint.

After Eden: Idolatry and Escapism

I have a further complaint against both the totalitarian and the nihilist accounts of our challenges: both of them are shallowly historicist. For them, the conditions of modernity create or embody a radical caesura or rupture in human history, wherein the discontinuities vastly outweigh the continuities; hence, to grapple with the modern condition requires in us a parallel break in our political thought.[12]

But Christians should resist these sorts of historicist narratives as superficial diagnoses of our situation. For Christian faith teaches that the vexation of our efforts is not simply a matter of historical contingency, potentially fixable by us. We live in history, to be sure. But we also live east of Eden and after Christ—in the epilogue, "after the Word," when everything has already occurred. The fall did not happen in 1277 with Archbishop Tempier's condemnations, nor when Scotus began to teach, nor in the Industrial Revolution; similarly, sin is not reducible to a pervasive philosophical commitment to ontotheology or consumerism. In fact we have lived after "the end of history" for a very long time: ever since AD 33. Some of the challenges we face are perennial, in this dispensation at least, and some of our difficulties are chronic. "Modernity" is not, that is, a properly theological category.

If we move in this direction, however, our problem becomes in one sense more profound: for it moves from the context of our time to humanity's perennial problems, at least as we have come stably to know humanity from its evolutionary emergence to today. Of

---

12. For a very good and stimulating discussion, see Jeffery Isaac, "Critics of Totalitarianism," in *The Cambridge History of Twentieth-Century Political Thought*, ed. Terrence Ball and Richard Bellamy (Cambridge: Cambridge University Press, 2003), 181–201.

course, the fact that this reframing makes the problem harder to resolve is itself an argument in its favor; for in this dispensation our problem is in fact intractable. The aim of this section is to see what, if this is true, we ought to do in light of it.

In fact, theological anthropology identifies the fundamental human problem, the crux of the postlapsarian human condition, precisely as a crisis of desire. Against the devotees of nihilism, human longing cannot be destroyed: we always want an infinite end, and as fallen creatures, our longing for an infinite end translates into a bad consumption of the world in which we will always want more, and when we do not get it, we seek satisfaction in bad ends, faulty goods, false gods. We end in idolatry. This is not to say that worldly goods are bad: as with any idolatry, there are genuine goods being pursued, goods needed for a flourishing life; but those goods become idols when we try to use them to satiate (which means, here, to suffocate) longings that they cannot properly fulfill—that is, our immaterial longings. Those who cry "nihilism" neither acknowledge the real and inescapable profundity of the problem, nor realize that that profundity itself is what should make us not despair.

There is no human solution to this—no sociopolitical arrangement, no technology, is deep enough. Nor—and here is the hope—will we ever leave this tortured longing behind. Humanity cannot apocalyptically dehumanize itself; God does not allow it.[13] We are stuck, graciously, in this damnably perilous state, and must learn how most fruitfully to inhabit it. In this situation most moral theology will be ascetical and therapeutic, dedicated to disenthralling us from the various determinate forms that idolatry and escapism take in our local cultural situation. Here, I propose, is the crux of one viable theological language for today.

---

13. See Peter Burnell, *The Augustinian Person* (Washington, DC: Catholic University of America Press, 2005).

Such an approach is, to my mind, especially vivid in Augustine's work, which has at its heart the idea that the human has (or better, is possessed by) infinite desire—that our longing is endless, that we are restless until we rest in God. Furthermore, Augustine's is a church theology, pedagogically focused, interested in cultivating believers' doxological capacities, their capacities for living a life of joyful praise to God.[14]

This approach is more functionally diagnostic and therapeutic than an approach concerned with nihilism. Here's how: much of what seems to be a new problem in modern life can be seen, following Pascal, as forms of *divertissement*. But such diversions are merely forms of boredom driven to desperation, attempting to escape its fundamental nature. The problem with this sort of solution to the quandaries of moral life is that it is endless. Such a strategy does not end in happiness, because it does not end. That is, it is not properly intelligible. It is bottomless: it has no aim, no goal beyond the negative one of evasion and deferral, and so, consumed as we are with not confronting our situation, we miss the intrinsic reality of whatever phenomenon or activity we are using for our *divertissement*.

But such avoidance will never make us happy. In fact, such an approach ends up making all of our pleasures hollow, for they serve us only as momentary pauses in the endless drama of manipulation we play with the world. Experience becomes wholly a matter of evasion, of avoiding the facts of our life, of escape, a way of staving off contemplating the emptiness of our lives in such situations; as Augustine once put it, "Such is the weakness of the flesh, such is the irksome nature of this life, that everything, however wonderful, ends in boredom."[15] Elsewhere, and more broadly, Augustine once quite

---

14. See Robert Dodaro, *Christ and the Just Society in the Thought of Augustine* (Cambridge: Cambridge University Press, 2004), Jason Byasse, *Praise Seeking Understanding* (Grand Rapids: Eerdmans, 2007), and various works by Lewis Ayres, John Cavadini, William Harmless, Michel René Barnes, and Michael Fiedrowicz.

insightfully described his own pursuit of such a goal in the *Confessions* as a process whereby he ended up making of himself a *regio egestasis*, a "desolate region," a desert.

This is all accurate as far as it goes, but it misses the social dimensions of the phenomenon, how such strategies of evasion can take different determinate shapes depending on the social context in which they exist, and how those several social situations habituate us in particular ways, into particular deformations of character. To better understand this, we can turn to Tocqueville, who described the fundamental worry as a rising "individualism" that encourages an isolation and anomie among citizens, and a lessening of the human capacities for true greatness and excellence. He saw that the mutually implicated rise of material wealth and equality in a democratic age do not make us significantly better, but may well instead encourage a certain kind of indifferent individualism in which each pursues a life of purely "private" pleasures in fundamental indifference to one another or to the commonweal. But Tocqueville's account, in turn, is not fully satisfactory either; its fixation on the diagnosis of individualism is, on its surface, at least, too narrowly and shallowly political. It does not attend to the psychic challenges we face. What is especially problematic about this individualism is how it gives us many new opportunities for avoidance—avoiding one another, avoiding ourselves, avoiding reality itself—and ultimately, on Christian terms, avoiding God.

In light of this analysis of individualism, the language of escapism and *divertissement* becomes useful: we are likely to use luxury, prosperity, and abundance not to inhabit life, but rather to avoid it. We use our abundance in the service of escapism, an escapism with fundamentally theological roots. This is finally idolatrous, for

---

15. Augustine, *Sermon* 243.8; see also *De civitate Dei*, 4.3, 15.

it reveals both that our attachment to certain goods in the world is always threatening to become a worshipful attachment, and that behind this counterfeit worship lies an even deeper idolatry, the commitment to the mastery of the world by the self, the desire to make the self its own god—or rather, to have no other gods before the self.

For all Tocqueville's indebtedness to past thinkers, he was convinced that new questions had to be asked. He went so far as to call for a "new political science" to understand the new age, with its new promise and new perils. But that new political science has not yet appeared. For it to do so, such a new political science would need to be a *theological*-political science, and in some important ways, an old one, at that. It must begin with the acknowledgement that human desire seems to have a functional "elective affinity," as it were, with infinite longing, longing of the sort traditionally associated with longing for God. This new theo-political science must begin from, if not a confession, at least an acknowledgment of the *bottomlessness* of human desire, the endlessness of our longings.[16] It must begin, that is, with our capacity for something like joy.

The details of how that might be undertaken are beyond the scope of this chapter. But this chapter cannot end without noting the ways that such a project also might find allies beyond Christian churches. I turn to the prospects for an "alliance for joy," across our pluralistic world, next.

An Alliance for Joy?

Let us take stock of what has been argued so far. If we think about the Christian life as a matter of cultivating joy, the task of the churches and derivatively of theology is to become spaces where we are

---

16. Even if we resist the reduction of the forms of those longings to a monochromatic language of desire.

graciously disenthralled from our various idolatries and taught to wait and live into the *distentio* of a sacramental life during the world. This also helps us to reframe our vision of the challenges confronting Christian life. In light of this reframing, our very many material blessings are for us a double-edged sword: while no one would seriously reject the great goods our ever increasing wealth and power allow us, we must become more cognizant of the characteristic vices attendant upon these blessings, the better to confront and resist them. Most obviously, our technological proficiency and material abundance enable in us a powerful tendency toward an attitude of avoidance. These vices mean that we do face a challenge with its own specific form—the challenge of a crisis of moral energy itself brought on by structural changes in the sociocultural order, changes that aggravate certain malformations of the psyche to which we are already, as fallen beings, prone. Such an understanding of our situation is superior to the two rival sorts of analyses of the challenges to Christian life in our world, those framing the worries in liberal terms as concerns with totalitarianism and oppression, and those framing the worries in aristocratic terms as concerns with nihilism, both because it is able to bring the whole spectrum and depth of the challenges we face more fully and vividly into view, and because it is more richly and organically in communion with traditional Christian orthodoxy.

As the above should make clear, so far this proposal has been wholly intra-Christian in character, concerned with the project of cultivating believers within the Christian churches. But it is not enough that churches do this; for themselves and for others, they must care about the social arrangements within which they exist. Churches cannot imagine that they are or will ever become the fundamental frameworks within which their parishioners live, or even understand their lives; the character of contemporary society makes such a conceit deeply implausible, and those who cling to it are simply unrealistic, or Amish.[17] The churches must work with others to ensure that, even in their own precincts, the work of healthy cultivation can go forward.

Fortunately, the idea of joy has appeal far beyond strictly Christian discourse. Many people outside of those churches also care about joy, or about things so analogous to joy as to be potential fellow travelers in this program. After all, many thoughtful people in advanced industrial societies today are better than this; indeed they share these worries, and are haunted by the too easy picture that these analogies entail. They are worried about these temptations, even as they feel them *as* temptations—in fact, precisely *because* they are worried about them as temptations. I recognize this, and my aim here is not to suggest that there is no hope for us, or that we are entirely lost. The bare fact that we can ask this question, and can feel the question as a worry about what we might become—and feel the temptation of despair as a temptation—speaks to the way that we are not without hope. (And why would one write if one did not have some hope?) And anyway, these are not concerns simply of grumpy antimoderns or antiliberals; thoughtful liberals like Jeffrey Stout or John Tomasi can and do recognize these dangers, and worry about them.[18] (Indeed, even a thinker as antithetical to Christianity as Nietzsche can share in these concerns.[19]) Charles Taylor has identified the general problem here to be one of trying to figure out how to have "fullness"

17. José Casanova, *Public Religions in the Modern World* (Chicago: The University of Chicago Press, 1994).

18. See Jeffrey Stout, *Democracy and Tradition* (Princeton: Princeton University Press, 2004), and John Tomasi, *Liberalism beyond Justice: Citizens, Society and the Boundaries of Political Theory* (Princeton: Princeton University Press, 2001).

19. See Robert Pippin's essay "Nietzsche on Naïve and Clumsy Lovers," in *Idealism as Modernism: Hegelian Variations* (New York: Cambridge University Press, 1997), and also, in a different vein, William James, "The Moral Equivalent of War," in *Writings: 1902–1910* (New York: Library of America, 1987), 1281–93.

in one's life; it is a problem endemic to our condition in late advanced industrial modernity. This essay is not an apocalyptic *cri de coeur* about the end of our moral world; it wants to be a more diagnostic, pedagogical, and ascetical inquiry about how we should best inhabit our condition. These worries, that is, are amenable to expression from quite diverse moral and religious standpoints. In sum: the category of "joy" is so general as to perhaps encompass, in an underdetermined manner, a great number of the more specific visions motivating many of the individuals and communities involved in our world today; and yet it still has enough content to perhaps be useful as a critical and constructive tool for immanent criticism, of traditions and movements and institutions.

Here I want to expand the program a bit and suggest that a focus on joy will, in part, aid us with those who are not Christian: in interreligious dialogue, and even in conversation with those of no particular religion. It does so because it helps keep a common goal at the center of general concern, and this goal can mobilize disparate actors to work together. A cross-traditional alliance for joy—properly (that is, expansively) understood—is possible, could be powerful, and if it comes it will come due to the ongoing conversation between movements like the Abrahamic traditions and the various versions of postmodernity. To accomplish such an alliance, and speaking pragmatically, we may well need multiple alternatives, as it is unlikely that one solution will suit all people. And of course there will be definite limits to unanimity of understanding and action, limits better conceived of as needing management than resolution; I will talk about those as well. But the crucial point is that such a pragmatic alliance may be of some use for us in coming decades, not just for Christian theological reflection and ecclesial practice, but for many others, in diverse ways, as well.

An *Oikonomia* of Joy?

As I said, I am not alone in offering the diagnosis of part 2. Many nonreligious critics identify a crisis in our capacity to experience joy, and the deforming effects of this crisis on our psychological, economic, and societal well-being. For them as for me, the idea of joy and delight seems increasingly fugitive in the thought patterns shaping and explaining our societies. And the experience of joy seems harder to understand in its proper terms, and so we "happen" upon it, which we may do less and less, ever more accidentally, ever more momentarily, before returning again to the flow of time onrushing. We consume what titillating amusements we will, and are sated; but we seem increasingly less able to delight, to pursue ecstatic, extrasubjective commitments. Tibor Scitovsky has aptly called this the "joyless economy"—one in which the distinct idea of joy has no place structurally, intellectually, and increasingly phenomenologically.[20] Such figures are promising candidates for allies in this campaign for joy.

Scitovsky was, in his time, a kind of *vox clamans in deserta*, who in turn echoed John Maynard Keynes, who in his essay "Economic

20. The literature on the problem of joy in the social sciences is rich; see Tibor Scitovsky, *The Joyless Economy: The Psychology of Human Satisfaction*, rev. ed. (New York: Oxford University Press, 1992), and his "How to Bring Joy into Economics," in *Human Desire and Economic Satisfaction: Essays on the Frontiers of Economics* (New York: New York University Press, 1986), 183–203. For another useful summary of the arguments, and a more recent overview of the literature—in economics, sociology, political science, and psychology—on happiness, see Carol Graham, *The Pursuit of Happiness: An Economy of Well-Being* (Washington, DC: Brookings Institution Press, 2011), esp. 55: "Utility defined simply by consumption choices equates the purchase of a Big Mac by an obese individual with that of a guitar string purchased by a professional musician." The point is *not* that such quantifiable attempts are pointless, but they can be misleading. See also Robert Lane, *The Loss of Happiness in Market Democracies* (New Haven: Yale University Press, 2001). On leisure time, see especially Douglas Kleiber, Gordon Walker, and Roger Mannell, *A Social Psychology of Leisure* (State College, PA: Venture Books, 2011). For a very good collection of essays on happiness by some leading figures, see Luigino Bruni and Pier Luigi Porta, eds., *Economics and Happiness: Framing the Analysis* (New York: Oxford University Press, 2005). See also Cass Sunstein and Richard Thaler, *Nudge: Improving Decisions about Health, Wealth, and Happiness* (New York: Penguin Books, 2009).

Possibilities for our Grandchildren" differentiated between the (contingent) problem of scarcity and the (permanent) problem of living a well-formed life.[21] More recently, the tradition of "behavioral economics," from Daniel Kahneman and Amos Tversky forward, and George Ainslie, moving to people like Richard Thaler and Cass Sunstein, have identified the ways in which neoclassical economics' psychology and axiology is not just philosophically flawed but empirically mistaken. Such thinkers suggest we can move beyond a focus on satiation, toward a concern with genuine eudaimonism, and that any such move would actually be in the direction of greater empirical realism.

The strengths of this work are manifold. Such scholars recognize the inadequacy of a purely consumptive moral anthropology (or at least we have some arguments in common on this matter, and ones that we may be able collectively to direct at those who disagree with us on this, to their vexation if not conversion). Furthermore, due to their nonreductionist picture of moral personhood, they are open to a more productive understanding of how religious visions can be functional participants in society. For political thinkers of even so decidedly secularist a bent as Jürgen Habermas, religion is a power (not the only one, but an important one) that should resist incorporation in the capitalist worldview. Some of these thinkers are even willing to say that religion also formulates positive claims that are, as it were, morally focusing—highlighting realities in the world that would otherwise go unnoticed—and morally energizing and inspiring—engaging those who apprehend such realities. Furthermore, it does *both* these things in ways that other sources of

21. See also James, "Moral Equivalent of War." Also, we need to appreciate the good of creativity—meaningful productive work. Robert Lane, *The Market Experience* (New York: Cambridge University Press, 1991) and Lorenzo Pecchi, *Revisiting Keynes: Economic Possibilities for Our Grandchildren* (Cambridge, MA: MIT Press, 2010).

moral deliberation, particularly much secular thinking, do not and perhaps cannot do.

Obviously, there are inevitable tensions between a frankly theological view such as the one offered in this chapter, and fundamentally secular views that are at least as common today. For example, the idea of happiness proposed in secular accounts may be too subjectivistic, individualist, or anthropocentric for Christians interested more centrally in joy. Real tensions may exist here, and need to be worked out over time. But this does not entail assertions of the sort that you occasionally hear from theological perspectives, namely, that "secularists don't really have a concept of joy." That is simply not true; most proximately, the post-Emersonian Romantic tradition, exemplified in this dimension especially by Whitman, may well have much to teach Christians about joy. The real and abiding and concrete differences between views will have to be confronted and managed, neither papered over nor rendered so insuperable as to warrant mutual indifference. There is no need for sheer unanimity of conviction as a precondition for collective action. Each partner in a genuine collaboration has their own interests to protect and advance as well as the interests of the collective; we can trust that there has never been any human organization so coherent as to obviate all recognition of the diversity of views within it. No one should expect, short of the eschaton, that all these divisions, and the differences in tactics and strategies that they entail, will go away. The coherence of this alliance is based primarily and essentially on a parallel recognition of the problem, on similar expressions of alarm and concern about the regnant picture of agency, even as those expressions of alarm and collection of concerns are themselves formulated in different vernaculars. The responses to these concerns will equally be diverse, though one hopes for significant collaboration on at least some fronts.

In any event, such an alliance seems possible, though not without its difficulties; and that is all I need to suggest now.

An Abrahamic Alliance?

Other, more proximate, possibilities for an alliance exist as well. Most notably I would propose that it is as regards these issues, and around this project of developing a nonapocalyptic cultural critique, that the Christian churches should pursue a long-term dialogue with a wide range of representatives of Islam, as the churches have so far failed utterly to do. This may well aid in the "liberalizing" of Islam that policy wonks talk so much about, by helping both sides work on improving their understanding of how to "be particular" in pluralistic public settings. But more than that rather condescending benefit, such a dialogue has much to teach Christians. It can teach us important things both indirectly, about the practice of the faith, in its similarities and dissimilarities with Judaism and Islam, and directly about the nature of joy itself, as that category (or its analogues in the traditions) is explored and articulated in other—very different but not absolutely dissimilar—traditions. (I suspect that practices such as Ramadan and keeping Shabbat could have a substantial deal to teach Christians about the cultivation of joy.) Such a dialogue has historical precedent; think of the Jewish-Christian dialogue after the Shoah, and all the good that has yet produced, not just in "understanding" between the two groups (though we ought not discount that), but also, for Christians at least, the deepening understanding of the profound "Jewishness" of proper Christian faith, and its self-understanding as a substory in the election of the people Israel. Perhaps we can turn to good use the current situation if this conversation gets under way. At the very least we ought seriously to try.

Of course, in the end this group of views would not culminate in simple harmony either, any more than would the engagement with nonreligious collaborators. Most prominently, different understandings among the Abrahamic traditions about the character of proper divine-human relation (christologically formed in Christianity, decidedly not in Judaism and Islam) and the nature of the human situation in this dispensation (and derivatively the shape of the human predicament herein) mean inevitably that serious and perduring differences will have to be accommodated in any such alliance.

Again, however, the fact that any Hegelian *Aufhebung* of all our differences is a very long way off, is no reason to refuse to forge an alliance (of Christian thesis and secular semi-antithesis, as it were) in the interim. Such differences as exist can be acknowledged frankly while yet pursuing a common aim of imagining a more morally sane and spiritually fruitful way of life than is currently widely available. Dialogically speaking, even the differences separating the communities could be made productive. And of course it will be a perennial temptation for any such Abrahamic alliance to alienate or estrange or demonize non-Abrahamic faiths and those of no faiths whatsoever. I do not think they need to do so—quite the opposite, in fact; and by working in good faith with others of differing beliefs, they may well be able to generate not just moral and intellectual understanding, and perhaps even greater tolerance as well.

Conclusion

Here I have tried to sketch how one (broadly Augustinian) tradition of Christian thought might go about imagining a theology built around joy, and I invite others to do the same. I think the structures and patterns and intellectual issues that joy brings to the surface, both in our economic and cultural moment and in Christian theology across history, do merit direct reflection from a variety of perspectives. I would urge others to see what they can do with it as well.

During the world, a way of life built around cultivating joy may well be our best route into recognizing and inhabiting our *distentio*, our experience of tantalizing incompleteness that we confess we exist in at present, while at the same time proclaiming that all will be healed in the eschaton. We must recognize both our own incompleteness, and the way that it tantalizes us. All of this is what the Christian churches' liturgies are meant to teach us—to give us the most exquisite training in longing we could imagine, in order to sculpt our souls into the right shape, to turn our minds toward contemplation of God's incomprehensible goodness, to stretch our hearts back to the size they were meant to be in the first place. It teaches us how to live faithfully, to be sure, and lovingly, but for our purposes most pointedly it teaches us how to live hope for joy.

A proper hope seeks a middle ground between the too-complacent apocalyptic immanentism of the resigned or self-righteous, and the too-complacent apocalyptic escapism of the embittered or smug. The liturgy anchors this view on its theology of history and creation, on its claim that history is not, during the world, finally literally legible, but only sacramentally so. Neither immanentists nor escapists can capture the true longings of humans, which inevitably transcend the mere satisfactions or anesthetics they impatiently advertise, and tell against them in our stubborn refusal to be satisfied with this dispensation, or satisfied in our dissatisfaction with it. True human flourishing will best blossom, I would argue, in a joy that is here and not here, now and not yet, ours and God's. God has made us for God's self, and our hearts are restless until they rest in God, so no worldly dispensation is adequate. Yet this dispensation matters; the violations and injustices here are not simply accidental or immaterial, and its joys and sorrows will finally be taken up into God and transformed into their full reality. It is out of this vision of the world, I believe, and the dispositions that it funds, that a theology of real joy, not debased consumerist satiation or fallen solipsistic happiness, might fruitfully begin.

Calling and Compassion: Elements of Joy in Lived Practices of Care

Mary Clark Moschella

The field of pastoral theology and care has been conceptualized as a form of religious response to human suffering. It is said that our research begins "at the point where human suffering evokes or calls for a religious response and sometimes at the point where a religious response is given and/or experienced."[1] In light of this widely shared understanding, it is not surprising that, with a few important exceptions,[2] joy is as understudied in this field as it is in the

---

1. Bonnie Miller-McLemore, "The Subversive Practice of Christian Theology," in *Christian Theology in Practice*, ed. Bonnie Miller-McLemore (Grand Rapids: Eerdmans, 2011), 143.

2. These exceptions include Peggy Way, *Created by God: Pastoral Care for All God's Creatures* (St. Louis: Chalice, 2005); and Angella Son, "Agents of Joy: A New Image of Pastoral Care," *The Journal of Pastoral Theology* 18, no.1 (2008): 61–85. Also see Volney P. Gay, *Joy and the Objects*

other theological disciplines represented in this volume. Given the power and pull of experiences of suffering that call forth a religious response, ranging from grief and trauma to poverty and prejudice, it is not easy to assert that human experiences of joy merit the focus of this field of study. Joy seems to be a comparatively lightweight topic, unrelated to human suffering and the need for pastoral care. Yet, as I have found in my research, lived experiences of suffering and joy are not polar opposites, but often close companions. In this field that "pursue(s) a participatory, performative, and proactive kind of knowing that stays close to the ground, attends to human agony and ecstasy, and attempts to relieve suffering,"[3] we have attended more to agony than ecstasy. "Making room for joy" in our research, teaching, and lived practices of care is necessary in order to more fully and deeply understand human life, and the range and power of religious responses that contribute to human flourishing.[4]

In order to advance this claim, I will begin with an exploration of the meaning of joy, using experiential and pastoral theological frameworks. This will be followed by a brief synopsis of the recent history of the field of pastoral theology and care, and an explanation of how joy became to a large degree absent from the conversation. Then I will offer a brief overview of my current research and analysis of the workings of joy in the lives of religious leaders and other caregivers, and my efforts to identify in their stories the ideas, theologies, practices, and habits that support joy and human flourishing. Finally, I will reflect upon the story of one of these

---

of Psychoanalysis: Literature, Belief, and Neurosis (New York: State University of New York Press, 2001).

3. Miller-McLemore, Christian Theology, 138.

4. This chapter draws on my current project, "Making Room for Joy," the title of which comes from two sources: Peggy Way, Created by God, 136–37; and Bill Clarke, Enough Room for Joy: The Early Days of Jean Vanier's L'Arche (New York: BlueBridge, 2007). I am indebted to the Henry Luce III Fellows in Theology Program for its support of this research. I also thank Carrie Doehring, Beverly Mitchell, and Douglas Clark for reading this chapter.

caregivers—the physician and human rights advocate, Paul Farmer—in some detail, focusing on references to vocation and compassion in his story, and advancing the case that calling and compassion are two elements of joy-full work that helps to increase human flourishing.

What Is Joy?

The noun *joy* has been defined as "the emotion of great delight or happiness caused by something exceptionally good or satisfying; keen pleasure; elation."[5] I think of joy as an embodied awareness of holy presence and extravagant love, an awareness that dawns upon us like grace. It carries a sense of the unexpected, of surprise. When C. S. Lewis wrote of his childhood in his memoir, *Surprised by Joy,* he noted that joy involves both memory and longing. "All joy reminds. It is never a possession, always a desire for something longer ago or further away or still 'about to be.'"[6] The experience of joy is something intensely felt, perceived as an ancient memory bubbling up from deep inside even while it also feels given, from some great beyond, an experience so unexpected and profound that one can only try to take it in. At the same time, joy leaves a lasting impression, one that comes to surface just as grief does, in the most ordinary of days. The experience of joy is not fleeting or shallow, but deep and striking. It is linked to some object of goodness or wonder.

Joy versus Happiness

Any attempt to define joy inevitably brings up the idea of happiness and the question of how they differ or overlap. While some make vociferous distinctions between the two, I view joy and happiness

5. Dictionary.com, http://dictionary.reference.com/browse/joy.
6. C. S. Lewis, *Surprised by Joy: The Shape of My Early Life* (New York: Harcourt Brace, 1955), 74.

as what William James might call "near relatives." James suggested that we could learn a good deal about a phenomenon by comparing it to other phenomena that are similar.[7] Happiness is similar to joy, though happiness suggests something milder, such as a good mood, good fortune, or a happy turn of events. The root *hap*, related to *happenstance*, suggests good luck. As Darrin McMahon puts it, "Happiness has deep roots in the soil of chance."[8] We are happy when things go our way, when we laugh and have fun, or when we have experience ourselves as fortunate.

In the United States we are familiar with the phrase *the pursuit of happiness* from the Declaration of Independence. This idea has long been associated with the private pursuit of material goods, such as in "the American dream." Today, the pursuit of happiness that is linked to prosperity can be seen in the near explosion of popular literature known as "happiness studies," and in the personal coaching for success industry that follows from it.[9] We can appreciate the goodness of human happiness, good mood, and even the pursuit of health, strength, and reasonable material well-being. Indeed, these experiences can give rise to a sense of gratitude, which sometimes leads to joy.

However, joy and happiness are not one and the same. Joy indicates something deeper, more embodied, more acute—it is akin to aliveness, or animating force. According to C. S. Lewis, "It must have the stab, the pang, the inconsolable longing."[10] Joy also signifies a broader and more transcendent sense of goodness, one that links not just to personal well-being, but also to the larger reality, and to a vision of broader human flourishing. Joy is both corporeal and

7. William James, *The Varieties of Religious Experience: A Study in Human Nature*, ed. Martin Marty (Hammondsworth: Penguin, 1982).
8. Darrin M. McMahon, *Happiness: A History* (New York: Atlantic Monthly, 2006), 11.
9. Ibid., 471–73.
10. Lewis, *Surprised by Joy*, 72.

corporate in this reading. It is linked to what we feel in our bodies and in our communities, our bodies of faith. Joy often arises out of deep interpersonal connections and the experiences of loving and being loved. It may also arise in communities of resistance to evil or injustice. It is something that is deeper for being shared. Joy has an expansive quality, a sense that there is enough, more than enough, goodness and love to go around.

Joy in Caregiving

In my investigation of joy as it is experienced and expressed in life-giving ministries of care, I have arrived at a pastoral theological description, rather than a definition, of joy. This description is provisional and particular, with no claim to being comprehensive or universal. In the narratives I have studied, joy comes down to this: to being awake and deeply alive, aware of the love and goodness of God, and mindful of the wondrous gift of life. This is a holistic awareness, involving thoughts, emotions, breath, body, and community. In these stories, joy emanates from love of neighbor and a sense of calling to stand with "the least of these," those who are socially, economically, or politically marginalized. This joy is not naïve, but seeing, and committed to caring.

Joy in pastoral ministries is magnified by the blessing of a sense of vocation that challenges one to step outside of one's self into relationships of care and communion. Heidi Neumark uses the term *ecstasy* to describe her experience of ministry in the South Bronx. She writes,

> *Ecstasy* comes from the Greek "*ek stasis*" and implies moving out of stasis, out of a set position. Of course, the word is used for spiritual transport, but it strikes me that the church ought to see its daily role as following a path of ecstasy, leaving behind all that is stagnant and staid and stepping out into the unknown, allowing ourselves to be displaced

as we enter into relationship with others in their space. Ecstasy, then, is not just interior communion with God but communion with our neighbor.[11]

It is the privilege of entering into deep communion with one's neighbor that holds the potential for enlarged and ecstatic joy for those engaged in caregiving ministries of diverse sorts.

What Joy Is Not

Along with this rather basic description of what joy is, I have also determined some things that joy is not. First, joy is not an escape from sorrow or a turning away from suffering. Ann Voscamp writes, "Joy and pain, they are but two arteries of the one heart that pumps through all those that don't numb themselves to really living."[12] Joy involves being awake and not numb, attuned to life in the present moment, with all of its sweetness as well as its sorrows. As caregivers well know, it is often while in the midst of working through a great sorrow that a glimmer of something like joy breaks through. Oddly, joy allows one to experience deep sorrow with less fear, because the precious and precarious dimensions of life present themselves as intertwined.

For the Romantics, who celebrated depth of feeling, the link between pain and joy was explicit. Coleridge, in his poem, "Dejection: An Ode" wrote, "Joy is the sweet voice, Joy the luminous cloud."[13] The intertwining of these deep feelings is evident to many of us. We can cry tears of pain and tears of joy. The Romantics understood joy as "subjective, intimate, and personal," and yet, also as an experience of something larger, transcendent. Carlyle used the

11. Heidi B. Neumark, *Breathing Space: A Spiritual Journey in the South Bronx* (Boston: Beacon, 2003), 31.
12. Ann Voscamp, *One Thousand Gifts: A Dare to Live Fully Right Where You Are* (Grand Rapids: Zondervan, 2010), 84.
13. Samuel Taylor Coleridge, cited in McMahon, *Happiness*, 285.

term *blessedness* to describe it.[14] Indeed, deep joy seems often tinged with spiritual force. It feels like the gift of God, in that it arrives on its own, connecting us to something larger than ourselves, something beyond us that we cannot quite fathom.

Second, joy is not a frill, an extra that we can do without. We do not live by bread alone.[15] Joy and some of its other "near relatives," such as wonder, beauty, and hope, can hold us and heal us when words and the usual distractions fail.[16] Whether encountered through nature, art, prayer, work, play, or human relationship, embodied experiences of joy in this sense of aliveness and awareness of the good are needed to feed and sustain us in sorrow, and to open in us pathways to the love of God and neighbor.

We also need joy in the sense of aliveness, awareness of both pleasure and pain in the body, for moral reasons, as Paula Cooey has pointed out.[17] The bodily awareness of pleasure and pain affects our capacity to empathize with other bodies in pain or in joy. We need this holistic aliveness in order to know right and wrong "in our bones," in order to be able to understand, know, and defend basic human dignity, and to promote human flourishing.

Finally, joy is not a distraction from broader social needs. Rather, as Jürgen Moltmann and numerous others have suggested, experiences of joy may help to fund movements of social resistance and

---

14. McMahon, *Happiness*, 290.

15. Deut. 8:3. Cited in a similar way in Thomas Troeger, *Wonder Reborn: Creating Sermons on Hymns, Music, and Poetry* (New York: Oxford University Press, 2010), 169.

16. For example, Marcia Mount Shoop, reflecting on her tragic experience of rape, speaks of her experience of "God's lure toward greater Beauty and a life of zest." Marcia Mount Shoop, *Let the Bones Dance: Embodiment and the Body of Christ* (Louisville: Westminster John Knox, 2010), 30.

17. Cooey writes, "Although it provides no single all-purpose solution, the body, in all its particularity and in its ambiguity as artifact in relation to sentience, serves nonetheless as one common condition shared by us all, a condition that relates us to all other sentience, a condition that further stands as an ethical criterion by which to assess the significance of our work, one from which we should not detour." Paula M. Cooey, *Religious Imagination and the Body: A Feminist Analysis* (New York: Oxford University Press, 1994), 128.

liberation.[18] The human longing for joy, especially when shared and nurtured in community, tends to irrupt into artistic and creative resistance to that which holds people back and restricts them. Such artistic expressions themselves often spur human responses, delight, and determination to work for change.[19]

It is this deeper understanding of joy as aliveness and attentiveness to the goodness of God[20] that I consider necessary, not ancillary, to the fullness of life, and to the abundance and flourishing that God desires for all people as well as for all creation.

Joy in Pastoral Theology and Care

In the academic field of pastoral theology and care, there is a decided need for joy. With the few important recent exceptions noted earlier,[21] it has been a neglected topic in our scholarship and teaching. Typically, in seminary or divinity school courses in pastoral theology, care, and counseling, students are taught very deliberately how to get a feel for what is bothering a person, how to see through surface matters to deeper issues and problems, how to stay with a person in sorrow and not try to fix it; how to explore theologies of suffering and accompany people on their journeys into questions of theodicy. Students are not usually taught how to sense a glimmer of gladness in someone's story or in some community's story, much less how to stay with it or help magnify an uplifting experience of God's grace.[22] The result of this is that we often train pastoral practitioners to become

18. Jürgen Moltmann, *Theology and Joy* (London: SCM, 1973), 26–28; Paula M. Cooey, *Willing the Good: Jesus, Dissent, and Desire* (Minneapolis: Augsburg Fortress, 2006), 8; Barbara A. Holmes, *Joy Unspeakable: Contemplative Practices in the Black Church* (Minneapolis: Fortress Press, 2004). See especially Holmes's reflections on the role of improvisational jazz in African American resistance movements, 174–77.

19. Mary Field Belenky, Lynn A. Bond, and Jacqueline S. Weinstock, *A Tradition That Has No Name: Nurturing the Development of People, Families, and Communities* (New York: Basic Books, 1999).

20. Way, *Created by God*, 138–52.

21. See n2.

focused on crises, such as illness, trauma, loss and grief, psychiatric illness, interpersonal violence, and disaster relief, to the degree that pastors become almost pain specialists.

While these various sorts of crises and need are all real conditions that rightly require pastoral care energies and skills, these conditions do not comprise the whole of human life. Nor does the duty to empathize with pain fulfill the whole range of pastoral care obligations in the cure of souls tradition.[23] Caregivers who look to be "carrying the weight of the world on their shoulders" may in fact be at least mildly depressed themselves, whether from second-hand stress or habits of neglecting their own well-being, their own souls. Thus they are unaccustomed, untrained, and perhaps unable to care helpfully for people who are longing for the fullness of healing, hope, joy, strength, or well-being. These experiences need nurturing and care as well, so that persons and communities can flourish and practice the love of God and neighbor with vitality and zest.

An example of the way in which experiences of joy are underacknowledged in pastoral ministry can be found in the pastoral prayers that are part of United Church of Christ worship services, where there is commonly a time set aside for congregants to offer their "celebrations and concerns." In many of these churches, worshipers are good at sharing their concerns, often describing their medical problems in almost gory detail, sharing their vulnerability, and receiving the sympathy, care, condolences, and prayers of the congregation. By contrast, when it comes to naming their blessings or joys, worshipers are much more reserved. Perhaps it is because

---

22. An exception to this can be found in the work of pastoral theologians who make use of narrative therapy and its strategies. See Christie Cozad Neuger, "Narrative Therapy," in *The Concise Dictionary of Pastoral Care and Counseling*, ed. Glenn H. Asquith Jr. (Nashville: Abingdon, 2010), 17–22.

23. William A. Clebsch and Charles R. Jaekle, eds., *Pastoral Care in Historical Perspective* (New York: Jason Aronson, 1994).

people do not wish to gloat, brag, or inspire envy. Yet when joys or celebrations are routinely abbreviated or even omitted, Paul's injunction to the Romans to "rejoice with those who rejoice, weep with those who weep" (12:15) goes only half heeded.

For the congregation, this is a twofold loss. First, there is the loss of the experience of enjoyment or pleasure that can come from sharing good news, both for the one who is speaking and for the faith community that is hearing it. The congregation misses out on a chance to truly celebrate and rejoice in the blessings that are named. This momentary joy in another's blessings could potentially be a source of solace or perspective for a person who, though struggling, might benefit from the experience of vicarious delight in another's well-being. But when the expression of blessings and thanksgiving (*eucharisteo*) is held back, the community loses out on the opportunity to marvel, wonder, rejoice, and honor the Giver of all gifts. Though hymns of joy may be sung, there is no connection made linking the joy of the liturgy and music to the realities of people's lives.[24]

The second loss involved in this practice of avoiding mention of celebrations or blessings, is the loss of important chances for theological reflection. If we were accustomed to going more fully into joy, really taking it apart and savoring every aspect of it, this might lead us to ask theological questions, questions such as, "Why me? Why have I been so blessed?" "Why have I been given this talent or this love or this bounty?" These questions might lead to discerning more deeply the meaning and purpose of our lives, and ways in which we might use our gifts, interests, and callings to further human flourishing. Just as pastoral counseling offers persons the opportunity to plumb the depths of their sorrows, it ought to be

---

24. On the need to link pastoral care and Christian worship, see Herbert Anderson and Edward Foley, *Mighty Stories, Dangerous Rituals: Weaving Together the Human and the Divine* (San Francisco: Jossey-Bass, 2001).

offering persons the opportunity to explore the heights and breadth of their experiences of grace, strength, goodness, beauty, and joy.

Experiences of joy, when explored more fully, offer avenues for a deeper understanding of God's goodness and love. When we are attentive and aware of God's presence in us and all creation, when we feel the joy of this firsthand, we are freed from the paralysis of fear or despair, if only temporarily. We can experience what Carrie Doehring calls the "ordinary goodness of life."[25] Moments like this, when they accumulate over time, strengthen and steady us, and teach us what is good, help us know what well-being looks and feels like. Such experiences free us to do our best creative work, and thereby enlarge the possibilities for proactive ministries that contribute to human flourishing. "Perhaps there is a reason you have been so richly blessed with such great intellect," one might say, for example, in a pastoral conversation. "Is there a use to which you can put your gift, that it might grow and expand?" It takes time to discern what might emerge, to find out where deep joy might lead. But in a world that sorely needs the strengths and gifts of every person, pastoral practitioners ought not to neglect the links between experiences of joy, expressions of gratitude to God, and the well-being of the faith community. To put it another way, joy is not a scarce resource to be hoarded or hidden, kept like a light under a bushel. Joy is rather more like the loaves and the fishes: when offered up and shared, it tends to multiply.

The paucity of attention paid to joy in this field is related to the ways in which pastoral care has been conceptualized in the last century. In part due to Anton Boisen and the Clinical Pastoral Education movement begun in 1925, pastors and chaplains in US seminaries have been taught to realize that healing and faith can

---

25. Carrie Doehring, *The Practice of Pastoral Care: A Postmodern Approach* (Louisville: Westminster John Knox, 2006), 140–42.

emerge "out of the depths" of sorrow and psychiatric illness, as they did for Boisen.[26] While this insight is critical, it does not address the possibility that spiritual wisdom and strength might also grow out of experiences of well-being, beauty, wonder, or creative endeavors.[27] Though Abraham Maslow's humanistic psychology pointed in this direction, as did Howard Clinebell's concept of "growth therapy,"[28] the pastoral care movement of the mid-twentieth century more broadly adopted psychodynamic models that were based on the study of pathology. Freud focused on curing neuroses, and the religion and health movement promised that ministers could do the same.[29] Freud famously told one patient that "much will be gained if we succeed in transforming your hysterical misery into common unhappiness."[30] Perhaps there is small wonder that joy has not been a central theme in pastoral theology and care.

If the goal of the field of pastoral counseling shrunk, in the mid-twentieth century, to individual psychotherapy to cure neuroses, this was soon challenged by the influence of various liberation theology movements that drove the development of broader theories of pastoral theology and ministry.[31] Due to this influence, the field has

26. Anton Boisen, *Out of the Depths: An Autobiographical Study of Mental Disorder and Religious Experience,* 1st ed. (New York: Harper, 1960). Also see Glenn H. Asquith, ed., *Vision from a Little Known Country: A Boisen Reader* (Journal of Pastoral Care Publications, 1992).

27. Paul Tillich, who was another important figure in the religion and health movement and the so-called New York Group, did address the importance of creativity. See Paul Tillich, *The Courage to Be* (New Haven: Yale University Press, 1952), 48. Allan Hugh Cole Jr. interprets: "To be spiritually active, or spiritually alive, one needs to create" (Allan Hugh Cole Jr., *Be Not Anxious: Pastoral Care of Disquieted Souls* [Grand Rapids: Eerdmans, 2008], 85).

28. Abraham Maslow, *Religions, Values, and Peak-Experiences* (New York: Penguin, 1994); and Howard J. Clinebell Jr., *Contemporary Growth Therapies* (Nashville: Abingdon, 1983).

29. Brooks Holifield, *A History of Pastoral Care in America* (Nashville: Abingdon, 1983); and Allison Stokes, *Ministry after Freud* (New York: Pilgrim, 1985).

30. Sigmund Freud, *Studies in Hysteria*, trans. and ed. James Strachey (New York: Basic Books, 1957).

31. Bonnie J. Miller-McLemore, "The Living Human Web: Pastoral Theology at the Turn of the Century," in *Through the Eyes of Women*, ed. Jeanne Stevenson-Moessner (Minneapolis: Fortress Press, 1996), 15.

shifted to a more communal, contextual paradigm.[32] While Anton Boisen had coined the term *the living human document* to signify the need for a pastor to study the actual person for whom one is caring, in 1996 Bonnie Miller-McLemore proposed the phrase *the living human web* to indicate the complex, interrelated social systems that pastoral theology and care must now address.[33] Family systems as well as "psychosocial systems" theories became central to our concern.[34] As various forms of social marginalization and injustice are becoming better understood, the challenges posed for students of pastoral care multiply, and the list of needed capacities for sensitive care continues to grow.[35] This more complex, contextual approach has greatly expanded and enriched pastoral theological models and repertoires of care.[36] At the same time, joy is still mostly missing in our ever-expanding course syllabi. It may be that instructors assume that human experiences of joy do not require any time, attention, or special skill to interpret or support.

This message inadvertently gets conveyed in various forms of training in ministerial formation. Students are told to know themselves, to know their own issues, so that they do not haplessly project these issues onto care seekers. Usually this means, "Know your wounds, your sore spots, your unprocessed losses." This is

---

32. Nancy Ramsay, *Pastoral Care and Counseling: Redefining the Paradigms* (Nashville: Abingdon, 2004).

33. Miller-McLemore, "Living Human Web."

34. For a historical explanation of these expanding and evolving models, see Donald Capps, *Giving Counsel: A Minister's Guidebook* (St. Louis: Chalice, 2001). Also see Larry Kent Graham, *Care of Persons, Care of Worlds: A Psychosystems Approach* (Nashville: Abingdon, 1992) and Valery M. DeMarinis, *Critical Caring: A Feminist Model for Pastoral Psychology* (Louisville: Westminster John Knox, 1994).

35. A good example of this expansion can be found in Sheryl Kujawa-Hollbrook and Karen Montagno's edited volume, *Injustice and the Care of Souls*, which catalogs various forms of social injustice and offers guidance for sensitive pastoral care in numerous diverse religious, cultural, geographic, and social contexts. Sheryl A. Kujawa-Holbrook and Karen B. Montagno, eds., *Injustice and the Care of Souls* (Minneapolis: Fortress Press, 2009).

36. Charles J. Scalise, *Bridging the Gap* (Nashville: Abingdon, 2003).

important. Those who offer caregiving ministry must tend to their own losses, needs, and wounds, lest they avoid listening to other people's pain or impose their neediness upon those for whom they attempt to care. John Savage notes that "you can enter the pain of another only at the level that you can enter your own."[37] I contend that the same principle also applies to experiences of embodied wonder, healing, hope, and joy. One can empathically imagine the deep joy of another only to the degree to which one can access the grace and love of God in one's own experience. We need to make room for joy in the formation of pastoral caregivers and clergy, as well as in pastoral research exploring joy and human flourishing at personal, social, and political levels.

The Study of Caregivers' Narratives

In my current research, I have taken a somewhat circuitous route to identifying pastoral theological themes and practices that create space for joy in caregivers' lives and ministries. I started by studying several first-person narrative accounts of religious leaders and caregivers, narratives that I read as joyful in the sense of deep aliveness or attentiveness. This was an attempt to "catch" joy in action, or more precisely, in the authors' reflections upon lived ministries in a variety of contexts. The authors do not all address the theme of joy per se, but their writings reveal the awareness of joy or ecstasy in that sense of "stepping out" toward the well-being and flourishing of the people they serve.[38] These accounts also describe life-giving or

---

37. John Savage, *Listening and Caring Skills in Ministry: A Guide for Groups and Leaders* (Nashville: Abingdon, 1995), 96.

38. Even in making this decision to study accounts of caregiving ministries that are fruitful and joyful, I am intentionally diverging from the more standard problem-centered approach. This choice of focus is in some ways analogous to positive psychology's intentional effort to study well-being rather than pathology. Duane Bidwell and Donald Batisky have begun to work along similar lines in their study of hope in children with end-stage renal disease, where they attend to "the hope-generating experiences and practices" of the children in their study and

fruitful ministries, and here I am relying on Henri Nouwen's distinction between fruitfulness and success.[39] Fruitfulness implies growth and flourishing, which cannot always be measured in quantitative terms.[40]

Though it was not intentional, I find that I have been drawn mostly to stories of life-giving and joyful ministries in contexts marked by poverty, struggle, or marginalization of some kind. This selection process developed in this way because of my interest in experiences of joy that occur "in the midst of chaos,"[41] in the midst of lived ministry, and not off in a retreat house or in a particularly privileged or protected setting. I also looked for accounts that in some way exemplify the meaning of pastoral care as "communicating the gospel to persons at the point of their need,"[42] as the pastoral theologian Carroll Wise once defined it. It is not an easy joy that I have been after, but a deep joy that knows sorrow and yet leans toward the light.

draw from these implications for revising pastoral praxis. See Duane R. Bidwell, "Eschatology and Childhood Hope: Reflections from Work in Progress," *The Journal of Pastoral Theology* 20, no. 2 (2010): 109–27; and Duane R. Bidwell and Donald L. Batisky, "Abundance in Finitude: An Exploratory Study of Children's Accounts of Hope in Chronic Illness," *The Journal of Pastoral Theology* 19, no. 1 (2009): 38–59.

39. Nouwen wrote, "A successful person has the energy to create something, to keep control over its development, and to make it available in large quantities. Success brings many rewards and often fame. Fruits, however, come from weakness and vulnerability. And fruits are unique. A child is the fruit conceived in vulnerability, community is the fruit born through shared brokenness, and intimacy is the fruit that grows through touching one another's wounds" (*Bread for the Journey: A Daybook of Wisdom and Faith* [San Francisco: HarperSanFrancisco, 1997]).

40. I also decided to exclude narratives related to the "prosperity gospel." For example, see Marla Frederick "Rags to Riches: Religion, Media, and the Performance of Wealth in a Neoliberal Age," in *Ethnographies of Neoliberalism*, ed. Carol Greenhouse (Philadelphia: University of Pennsylvania Press, 2009).

41. Bonnie J. Miller-McLemore, *In the Midst of Chaos: Caring for Children as Spiritual Practice* (San Francisco: Jossey-Bass, 2007).

42. Carroll Wise, *The Meaning of Pastoral Care* (New York: Harper and Row, 1966), cited in Emma J. Justes, *Hearing beyond the Words: How to Become a Listening Pastor* (Nashville: Abingdon, 2006), 8.

These accounts include Heidi Neumark's *Breathing Space*,[43] the story of her ministry for twenty years in the South Bronx; Gregory Boyle's *Tattoos on the Heart*,[44] his reflection on ministry with gang members and their families in East Los Angeles, where he founded "Homeboy Industries," an organization that has in the last thirty years provided jobs for over forty thousand ex-gang members; Henri's Nouwen's book *Adam*,[45] a reflection on his work in the L'Arche community in Toronto, along with current studies and reflections on the L'Arche communities around the world, and their sustained caregiving ministries to and with persons with severe dis/abilities; Desmond Tutu, in particular, his narrative coauthored with his daughter, Mpho Tutu, *Made for Goodness*,[46] a story of memories and reflections upon the struggle against apartheid; and finally (expanding the definition of caregiving ministries), Paul Farmer, one of the founders of Partners in Health, through reflections in his own writings as well as his comments cited in *Mountains beyond Mountains*,[47] a close study of Farmer's early work in medical ethnography and care in Haiti. I have tried to interrogate these narratives in order to identify in them some of the key themes, theological ideas, and practices that create space for joy in these caregivers' experiences and in their various ministries of care.

The main themes and practices that I have found in these accounts include the following: a sense of calling or vocation, along with a conviction that one is fulfilling the vocation; a practice of presence, attentiveness to moments, people, and the good; a capacity for feeling

---

43. Neumark, *Breathing Space.*
44. Gregory Boyle, *Tattoos on the Heart: The Power of Boundless Compassion* (New York: Free Press, 2010).
45. Henri Nouwen, *Adam: God's Beloved* (Maryknoll, NY: Orbis, 1997).
46. Desmond Tutu and Mpho A. Tutu, *Made for Goodness: And Why This Makes All the Difference* (New York: HarperOne, 2010).
47. Tracy Kidder, *Mountains beyond Mountains* (New York: Random House, 2004).

gratitude and wonder; a habit of collaboration with and connection to colleagues and communities of care; the practice of compassion; habits of theological reflection and self-awareness; and, finally, a tendency to notice and perceive beauty, strength, and goodness in God, in human beings, or in creation. Not all of these themes, capacities, and practices were evident in all of the accounts. But a good number were discernible in each.

I will now turn to the story of Paul Farmer, highlighting two of these themes: the first, a sense of calling; and the second, a practice of compassion. These are two of the elements in his story that seem to help him gain access to a deep sense of hope, even in circumstances that are often daunting and sometimes painfully discouraging. Farmer's commitment to the good, and the joy that it gives him, help to motivate and propel forward his important work that directly supports human flourishing through his calling to a medical mission serving the poorest of the poor.

Paul Farmer's Story

In *Mountains beyond Mountains,* journalist Tracy Kidder describes the early work of Paul Farmer, a physician who began conducting medical ethnography in Haiti in 1983 in order to understand better how to offer effective care to people living in Mirebalais, Haiti, and the surrounding arid mountains. Farmer eventually became a medical professor as well as one of the founding directors of Partners in Health, a highly effective international organization devoted to treating HIV/AIDS, eradicating drug-resistant tuberculosis, as well as treating other diseases and lifting the standard of living among the world's poorest populations. Partners in Health works to provide basic medical care and alleviate poverty in Haiti, Lesotho, Malawi, Rwanda, Mexico, Peru, Russia, Kazakhstan, and in the United States as well.[48] This work takes place in prisons, in rural villages, and in urban centers.

According to Kidder's account, Farmer was brought up in a large, quirky, Catholic family that lived alternately in a bus, a boat, and a trailer park. His father was a force of nature, demanding that the children work hard to support his many projects, by cleaning the bilge of their home, for example. A bright child, Paul threw himself into schoolwork and extracurricular activities. He was not particularly interested in religion.

It was as a college student at Duke in 1980, when Archbishop Oscar Romero was killed, that Farmer first read liberation theology. And it was through his acquaintance with some of the nuns working in migrant labor camps in North Carolina, not far from Duke, with Friends of the United Farmworkers, that Farmer first met Haitian immigrants working on tobacco farms. He was shocked by the conditions in which the Haitian laborers were living, and he began to think of them as the poorest of the poor, or in his words, "the shafted of the shafted."[49] He began to study medical anthropology, and was particularly influenced by the theories of Rudolf Virchow, who Farmer understood to have had a comprehensive vision that linked "pathology, social medicine, politics, and anthropology."[50] Farmer then spent part of a year in Paris, where took one of the last courses offered by Claude Levi-Strauss, while working as an au pair and becoming fluent in French.

Before he began his studies at Harvard Medical School, Farmer won a scholarship that enabled him to travel to Haiti for the first time. He began conducting medical ethnography in Mirebalais in 1983. His interviewing took him to the surrounding mountain

48. For more details, see the Partners in Health website, www.pih.org.
49. Kidder, *Mountains beyond Mountains*, 63.
50. Ibid., 61.

communities, where he got to know many of the people. In one of these communities, Cange, he noted that the roofs of huts were made of banana-bark thatch and patched with rags, because the people could not afford tin. The poverty and sickness that Farmer witnessed here were both extreme and, he noted, community wide.[51] Moved by the faith of the people in Cange, Farmer was drawn back toward Catholicism and specifically liberation theology. The peasants seemed to have their own version of it. "Everybody else hates us," they'd tell him, "but God loves the poor more. And our cause is just."[52]

As he was formulating a vision for his life's work, Farmer took for his motto one theological idea: "O for the P," as he calls it, shorthand for God's preferential option for the poor. He also learned a Haitian proverb, "Bondye konn bay, men li pas konn separe," which translates as "God gives but doesn't share." Farmer interprets this to mean, "God gives humans everything we need to flourish, but he's not the one who is supposed to divvy up the loot. That charge was laid upon us."[53] In a very pragmatic way, Farmer has devoted himself to redivvying up the loot of health care, on a worldwide scale. Over the last thirty years, his work with Partners in Health has directly refuted the once prevailing medical wisdom that it simply was not practical or possible, "viable" or "sustainable" to treat certain infectious diseases, such as HIV/AIDS, in poor countries.[54]

In 2013, Farmer's work is still guided by his conviction of a preferential option for the poor. He now considers health care a human right, and has written extensively in this topic.[55] The goal that he and Partners in Health now embrace is a bold one: "global health

51. Ibid., 77.
52. Ibid., 78.
53. Ibid., 79.
54. Haun Saussy, "Introduction: The Right to Claim Rights," in Paul Farmer, *Partner to the Poor: A Paul Farmer Reader*, ed. Haun Saussy (Berkeley: University of California Press, 2010), 5–11.
55. See, for example, "Rethinking Health and Human Rights: Time for a Paradigm Shift," in Farmer, *Partner to the Poor*, 435–70.

equity."[56] Farmer is not a lone heroic figure, but one who works together with a committed and growing group of associates and supporters with diverse talents, resources, and gifts.[57] Yet Farmer's particular love of medicine, his zeal for treating the patient who is in front of him, and his drive to find the best possible treatments and most intelligent systems of delivery for the poorest of the poor, captured my attention.

What, you might ask, has joy got to do with it? Farmer does not present himself as a happy-go-lucky type, but his writings and comments express the vibrant and deeply alive quality of joy. What gives him joy? Is it the hope that the goal of global health equity will soon be realized? Is his joy in the successes that Partners in Health has had, such as in treating large numbers of people with HIV/AIDS in Africa, or in the recent construction of a gleaming new teaching hospital in Mirebalais? Is it in treating that one patient before him? Or in teaching the many medical students who come to learn from him? Or does it come from rising to the intellectual challenge of seeing the connections between poverty, disease, resources, and needs, and mobilizing people to meet them?

In Farmer's writings, it becomes clear that the joy of this work does not come from naïveté about the magnitude of the problems besetting the goal of global health equity, or any sense that there is currently enough political will to achieve this goal. Farmer is well aware of the stark conditions on the ground, and he is clearly saddened, particularly by what he calls "stupid deaths," premature deaths that could be prevented with appropriate medical care and resources. Farmer does celebrate even the small improvements and accomplishments, though he is also aware of failures, continuing

---

56. Paul Farmer, "Two Years after the Quake," Partners in Health, http://www.pih.org/blog/two-years-after-the-quake.
57. The most well-known of the cofounders of Partners in Health is Jim Yong Kim, current president of the World Bank.

needs, and is driven to evaluate and improve the health-care systems that PIH designs. Farmer seems to be able to allow the pressing needs of people to spur him on, rather than drag him down into pessimism or despair. For example, in offering a New Year's message in January 2012, he spoke of gratitude and determination, and of the need to share his uplift with others even if it might be only "to give myself hope and to spur all of us to launch, continue, or finish some ambitious and urgently needed projects." He calls hope the "secret sauce."[58]

Farmer's hope goes further, though, in that he approaches the work with a focus on resources, insistently challenging the notion of scarcity, in spite of all that he has seen. He asserts that efforts to treat one disease are inevitably linked to efforts to treat other diseases, provide jobs, and alleviate poverty. He sees interrelationships between all of these and claims that resources directed toward one project will not take away resources from another, but help lift these interrelated projects.

Farmer writes, "None of our ambitious programs should be curbed by the pernicious notion of goodness as a limited commodity. We need to expand the notion of good and the notion of excellence and the idea that one flagship project might raise the aspirations of all of our efforts."[59] He expands upon this notion of meliorism with a citation from one of William James's talks to teachers. James said,

> Spinoza long ago wrote in his *Ethics* that anything that a man can avoid under the notion that it is bad he may also avoid under the notion that something else is good. He who acts habitually *sub specie mali*, under the negative notion, the notion of the bad, was called a slave by Spinoza. To him who acts habitually under the notion of the good he gives the name of freeman. See to it now, I beg you, that you make freemen of your

---

58. Farmer, "Two Years after the Quake."
59. Ibid., 7.

pupils by habituating them to act, whenever possible, under the notion of the good.[60]

I think that the joy in Paul Farmer's story is related to this, that he works under a notion of the good, a vision of the good that he can imagine. He does not believe that good is scarce. Though the good—in terms of resources, medical technology, training, teaching, and direct service—is not yet fully harnessed for human flourishing, Farmer believes that it can be and directs his life energy toward that goal. Farmer is tuned in to the possibilities for the good in the demanding and sometimes overwhelmingly sad work in which he and his numerous partners around the world are engaged. What are the ideas, habits, and practices that contribute to Farmer's joy and commitment to the good? Two themes that stand out in my reading are a sense of vocation and a practice of compassion.

Vocation

In my study of caregivers whose stories express or evoke deep joy, a strong sense of vocation is one of the consistent themes. This is not surprising in that many of the other individuals whose stories I studied were or are ordained Christian clergymen or -women. However, what stands out in their stories is not just a sense of calling to the ministry, but a conviction that they are precisely where they belong, doing the exact work to which they are called. In these writings, there is a sense of freedom and delight in the conviction that one is called to a particular people or place, and that one is answering that call, fulfilling his or her purpose. The delight seems to come, for these individuals, not from pride in great accomplishments, but from the actual engagement in the work, involving the exercise of talents

---

60. Ibid., 10, citing William James, *Talks to Teachers on Psychology* (Cambridge, MA: Harvard University Press, 1983), 113.

and the freedom to "step out" from stasis into understanding the worlds of others, particularly others who live on the social, economic, or political margins of life.

Psychological Analyses

What is vocation? Psychologically, it has been analyzed from at least two different points of view. Positive psychologists, who are attempting to study human well-being, often revert to theological language when they describe what it is like for people to be engaged in fulfilling work. For example, they point out that when people find a way to engage in work that requires their strongest skills, abilities, talents, and virtues, the work starts to feel more like a calling than a job. Positive psychologists assert that all people have a set of talents and personal strengths dubbed their "signature skills."[61] These skills are said to provide "intrinsic motivation."[62] This is a kind of delight that comes from exercising these skills or talents for their own sake. In trying to imagine examples of this, we might think of artists or musicians first. Annie Dillard describes a joyful painter who began painting because he liked the smell of paint.[63] There are many other activities (and related materials) in which diverse individuals find particular pleasure. I think for example of the man who was head of the moving van crew that packed and moved my family's belongings to Connecticut. I watched him pack the china with amazement. He was caught up in a rhythm of folding each plate into a thick packet of newsprint, then securely tucking it into a padded spot in the box. "I love it," he told me, smiling, not missing a beat.

---

61. Alan Carr, *Positive Psychology: The Science of Happiness and Human Strengths*, 2nd ed. (New York: Routledge, 2011), 70–78.
62. Ibid., 125.
63. Annie Dillard, *The Writing Life* (New York: Harper and Row, 1989), 70.

The sense of deep delight or "flow"[64] that can come when one is absorbed in work one loves and at which one is good, is enhanced, it is claimed, when the person performing the work is convinced that he or she is contributing to some larger cause or purpose. So, a parent might take joy in working hard if he or she is convinced that it will help give a child a better life; or, one might get great joy out of building houses for Habitat for Humanity (especially if one knows how). When these two things combine—that is, when one is using one's strongest skills, talents, or virtues, and one is convinced that one is contributing to a larger good—the work starts to feel expansive and richly rewarding. That sense of fulfilling one's precise calling, especially when it is linked to a sense that one is increasing the greater good, is what brings about a deeper sense of purpose that we might call joy.

This analysis from positive psychology raises several questions for pastoral theologians, some of which I have entertained elsewhere.[65] The most obvious, perhaps, is whether it matters that one's work is actually contributing to a larger good, or only that one thinks this is the case. We could imagine, for example, people experiencing a sense of joy and purpose in working with others in a political campaign, on either side of an issue. We cannot conclude that such experiences always lead to the increase of human flourishing.

Authors in another branch of psychology, the psychology of religion, take a different tack in studying joy. Classifying joy as an emotion, they suggest that joy, wonder, and interest are linked. They find that when people experience one of these three emotions, the other two shortly follow. Further, it is claimed that, joy, wonder, and interest help mobilize the capacity for compassion and empathy.

64. Mihaly Csikszentmihalyi, *Flow: The Psychology of Optimal Experience* (New York: Harper Perennial Modern Classics, 2008).

65. Mary Clark Moschella, "Positive Psychology as a Resource for Pastoral Theology and Care: A Preliminary Assessment," *The Journal of Pastoral Theology*, 21, no. 1 (2011): 1–17.

As Robert Fuller notes, "Wonder redraws our world of concern, establishing true mutuality with a wider sphere of life."[66] Another way of putting this is to say that wonder, joy, and interest help us focus on larger questions and, therefore, can keep us engaged in caring for wider spheres of life. Fuller points to an example of this is in the life of John Muir, whose sense of wonder, awe, and joy in the beauty of nature not only fed his own spiritual longings throughout his life, but also inspired his key role in the establishment of the national parks system in this country. Rachel Carson is noted as another figure whose strong sense of wonder led to her important and influential writing, which laid the groundwork for the environmental movement.[67] In the lives of these two individuals, a strong sense of wonder, interest, and joy significantly motivated their estimable contributions, not just to human flourishing, but also to the flourishing of the earth.

The insights from these two branches of psychological study shed light on the role of both calling and compassion in caregivers' stories. Though Paul Farmer is neither theologian nor religious leader, his personal writings and reflections suggest that he has found his calling in medicine, specifically in treating poor patients and in insisting that they be treated with dignity and respect. He has been using his considerable intelligence and skill to write articles and books documenting treatment strategies, evaluating their effectiveness, and creating a feedback loop between service, research, and teaching, which he compares to "praxis."[68] When thinking about his story in light of the strengths' research, we might start to suspect that

---

66. Robert C. Fuller, *Wonder: From Emotion to Spirituality* (Chapel Hill: University of North Carolina Press, 2006), 95; also see Herbert Andersen, "Witnessing Wonder," in Herbert Anderson and Bonnie Miller-McLemore, *Faith's Wisdom for Daily Living* (Minneapolis: Augsburg Fortress, 2008).
67. On Muir, see Fuller, *Wonder,* 42–53; on Carson, see ibid., 101–9.
68. Paul Farmer, *Partner to the Poor,* 565.

Farmer's intellectual strengths, together with his professional training and his clinical skills, would almost require him to take on such prodigious and varied work in order for him to feel fully alive and enthusiastically engaged. Further, his genuine curiosity and interest in medicine and the complexity of global health care help keep him engaged in thinking about the larger and more complicated questions related to "divvying up the loot" and finding ways to deliver needed services. In his story, we find evidence of strong moral convictions and vocational clarity, not in the sense of a religious vocation, but in the sense of a well-fitting match between his skills, interests, and convictions, and the work in which he is engaged. Further, we can see how this combination of theological values and professional strengths help him to live into his "vision for his life's work" with zeal and commitment to a greater good.

Compassion

Now, let's return to the second feature of his story noted earlier—the capacity for and the practice of compassion. Here Robert Fuller's finding (that being engaged in something that holds one's interest leads naturally to a capacity for greater compassion and empathy) is germane. Certainly this point is salient for pastoral theology and care, in that it suggests a natural association between joy and a genuine feeling of care or compassion.

Compassion is another key theme in Farmer's story, as is illustrated in an incident that Tracy Kidder and others describe. In 2000, a Boston physician and Partners in Health volunteer named Serena Koenig was working in Haiti, treating a boy named John who was found to have a rare form of nasopharyngeal cancer. It was a treatable condition, but it could not be successfully treated in the hospital in Haiti, so Koenig persuaded her colleagues at Massachusetts General Hospital to provide free care for the boy. However, by the time

Koenig went back to Haiti to transport the boy, John was too ill to travel on a commercial flight. Koenig decided, with Farmer's approval, to airlift John out on a Medivac flight. John was brought to Massachusetts General, where it was determined that the cancer had spread to the bone, that he was in extreme pain, and that there was now no chance for his cure. Instead, John was given palliative care, and his mother was flown in to be with him until he died.

When Farmer was later asked why Partners in Health went to such great lengths to save this one child, spending close to $20,000 on the airlift alone, he answered, "Because his mother brought him to us, and that's where he was, in our clinic."[69] The wisdom of this move could certainly be challenged from the point of view of those doing cost-benefit analysis (especially since the patient died, though the progress of his illness could not have been determined with the technology available in Haiti at the time). Yet this story illustrates the way in which compassion is integral to the philosophy of Partners in Health physicians. Theirs is an approach that says that the person in front of you is no less important than any other person. If it is possible to treat that person in front of you, then that is what you do. "If it were me in this situation, what would I want done?" is a question often cited.[70] This kind of compassion might also be interpreted as loving one's neighbor as one's self.

Paul Farmer is well aware that he cannot treat every patient, but he is determined to give his full attention to those he does treat, and to stay rooted in the experience of human care and compassion. "That's when I feel most alive," he told Kidder, "when I'm helping people."[71] Farmer's vocational clarity and his practice of compassionate medicine contribute to his own joy, his sense of deep aliveness, as

69. Ibid., 287.
70. Ibid.
71. Ibid., 295.

well as the joy and well-being of the many patients and communities that Partners in Health serves.

Theological Reflection

Gregory Boyle, another caregiver in my study, writes, "Compassion is always, at its most authentic, about a shift from the cramped world of self-preoccupation into a more expansive place of fellowship, of true kinship."[72] The practice of compassion opens us out to the spacious joy of recognizing our connection to each other, realizing that we are not alone or limited to our own resources. It is this expansive place of fellowship, made known in community, that can help motivate and sustain commitments to human flourishing.[73]

Compassion and calling are seeds of joy that are fed and watered by the abundant love and goodness of God. They are not merely psychological dynamics, but also spiritual experiences, through which the divine goodness, presence, and love are made known. It is no surprise, then, that Farmer's story, like the others I was drawn to for their depth of joy, is a story of love for the poor, a story of kinship with those whom the world considers the least and the lost. It is in response to the gospel proclamation of good news to the poor that Farmer and others find the freedom to live "under the notion of the good," the abundant goodness of God. And it is in responding with compassion to those who are marginalized that many find the joy of true kinship, mutual interest and connection, the wonder of human love.

Farmer's is also a story of love for life, a story "filled with livingness."[74] The story reveals not only Farmer's sense of calling, his

---

72. Boyle, *Tattoos on the Heart*, 77.
73. For a study of commitment to the common good, see Laurent A. Parks Daloz, Cheryl H. Keen, James P. Keen, and Sharon Daloz Parks, *Common Fire: Leading Lives of Commitment in a Complex World* (Boston: Beacon, 1996).
74. Jürgen Moltmann, *Ethics of Hope,* trans. Margaret Kohl (Minneapolis: Fortress Press, 2012), 57.

gifts, and talents, but also his wholehearted and creative engagement of these gifts. In responding to his calling Farmer discovers, not scarcity, but abundance, abundance that only needs to be redivvied, so that humanity can flourish. Moltmann reminds us that God's abundance is revealed in the imagination and courage to see the world, not just as it is—full of injustice—but as it could be, transformed.[75] God's gift of joy, experienced as deep awareness and aliveness, as well as calling and compassion, illumines and creates pathways towards human flourishing.

Many years ago, the Presbyterian pastor and author, Frederick Buechner, noted that "the place God calls you to is the place where your deep gladness and the world's deep hunger meet."[76] This is a definition of calling still worth communicating to students who come to divinity school with a vague sense of calling and a deep desire to help change the world. Their dreams of making a difference are not too big, for we live in a world that needs our aliveness and compassionate attention, on personal, communal, and global levels.[77] We need to nurture students as they try to discern their own joyful and life-giving vocations, so that they themselves can blossom and flourish, even as they use their gifts to meet the world's deep needs.

God's gift of joy, whether in caregiving ministries or in other realms of faithful living, is not a superfluous or trivial matter. Joy is not an extra thing to add on to a ministry or a life, like icing on a cake. Joy may seem unrelated to the seriousness of real work for human flourishing, but it is not. Rather, the absence of joy is a sign of diminished or constricted life, as Volney Gay has noted.[78]

75. Moltmann writes, "In hope we link far-off goals with goals within reach. What is last of all gives meaning to the next-to-last. So in the imagination of hope there is always a superabundance of what is hoped for" (ibid., 3). While hope and joy are distinct gifts, they are not unrelated.
76. Frederick Buechner, *Wishful Thinking: A Theological ABC* (New York: Harper and Row, 1973), 95.
77. Sharon Daloz Parks, *Big Questions, Worthy Dreams: Mentoring Emerging Adults in Their Search for Meaning, Purpose, and Faith*, rev. ed. (San Francisco: Jossey-Bass, 2011).

Joy is a critical component of attentive and engaged human living. Joy enlivens and sustains us, and flows through our commitments to life-giving work and vocations. And it opens up pathways toward compassion and connection, otherwise known as the love of God and neighbor. Joy is right at the heart of what it means to be fully alive, and right at the tender heart of God.

78. Gay, *Joy and the Objects of Psychoanalysis*; see especially chapter 1, "Neurotic Suffering as the Absence of Joy," 19–54.

$$6$$

The Crown of the Good Life: A Hypothesis

Miroslav Volf

"To[1] miss the joy is to miss all," wrote Robert Louis Stevenson in his essay "The Lantern-Bearers" (1887).[2] No matter what we possess or experience and irrespective of how we act, if we miss joy we have missed all. Stevenson's bold and perhaps exaggerated claim is a distant and garbled echo of the accolade the Master in one of Jesus' parables

---

1. A version of this essay was first published in the Big Questions Online series curated by the John Templeton Foundation. I am grateful to the foundation for awarding the Yale Center for Faith and Culture the planning grant for the theology of joy; to the dozens of participants in our exploratory discussions of joy who all helped clarify for us the character of joy and its relation to the good life; to researchers at the Center—Justin Crisp, John Hartley, Ryan McAnnally-Linz, and especially Matthew Croasmun—for conversations and comments on written versions of this text.
2. Robert Louis Stevenson, "The Lantern-Bearers," in *The Lantern-Bearers and Other Essays*, ed. Jeremy Traglown (New York: First Cooper Square Press, 1999), 234. In "On a Certain Blindness in Human Beings" (in *On Some of Life's Ideals* [New York: Henry Holt and Co., 1912], 16), William James quotes from Stevenson's essay extensively and with approval.

gave to the good and trustworthy servant: "Enter into the joy of your master!" (Matt. 25:23). Here joy is *the* reward for a job well done and a hefty return on investment achieved, which is to say, the reward for a life well lived. The best benefit the Master is able to bestow and the servant could hope to receive is *joy in a world of joy*!

Should joy, all its delights notwithstanding, get such a pride of place in human life? Can what seems like an elusive feeling pull toward itself the noblest human strivings? Might not joy be to a good life what sugar is to nutritious and richly flavored food? Isn't joy rather much like what we today call happiness—a feeling of pleasure—and therefore a dubious candidate for the good life? According to the *Oxford English Dictionary* (2014) joy is just that, with some intensity added: "A feeling of great pleasure and happiness." But defining joy as a "feeling of great pleasure and happiness" is like describing champagne as a bubbly liquid, but forgetting all about its golden color, whiffs of ripe pear and fresh baked bread in its aroma, or traces of apple, vanilla, yeast, and nuts in its flavor, and, of course, its capacity to intoxicate.

What are some smells and flavors of joy? To spare you disappointment, I should note that I am not about to take you to a joy-tasting event. As it turns out, no such event can be set up. You can't swish little sips of various joys on your emotional palate; as I will note later, when joy comes, it mostly supervenes on the complex system of thoughts, actions, dispositions, practices, situations, events, and so on, that together can be summed up in two phrases: *life being led well* and *life going well*. Instead, I am taking you into a "laboratory" where I hope to identify and analyze joy's component parts. For reasons that I don't fully understand, joy, an emotion that ranks close to the top in the hierarchy of emotions, is also the least studied. Psychologists and philosophers don't bother much about it; religious scholars, as distinct from preachers and spiritual masters, mention it in passing; even Wikipedia, which has entries on everything, has what amounts to a disambiguation page instead of an article on joy. I trust that by the time our somewhat arduous lab work is done, you will be persuaded that joy is much richer than the feeling of happiness, even great happiness, and that the authentic joy, though not itself the good life, *is the emotional substance and manifestation of the good life.*

Sketching Joy

What is joy?

First of all, joy is an emotion, not a mere feeling. Feelings are bodily reactions, and they have causes: a feather under my nose causes a tickle, for instance. Emotions are active responses, and they have objects; a child is born, and I rejoice *over* the event. That said, joy certainly does involve positive feelings. It is a positive affective response to having something good happen to those for whom we care or, as Thomas Aquinas writes, joy is a response to having been "united" with what we love. Depending on the intensity of the feeling, joy can range from exuberance (say, over one's team winning the World Cup) to calm delight (say, over a quietly sleeping child).

Joy involves the *construal* of the object of joy as good; it is tied to how I perceive things rather than to what things are in themselves. I can perceive an event—the birth of a child, for instance—as something good or as something unbearably burdensome. I will rejoice over it only if I perceive it as good. Equally importantly, joy construes its objects as wondrous, unowed; joy wells up in me when I see myself or those for whom I care as having had a good fortune or having been blessed. For instance, I rejoice over a bonus but not over getting regular pay (unless I consider myself blessed to have a job at all), or I rejoice over creation if I construe it as a wonder and a gift but not if I think of it as mere nexus of causes and effects.

Related as it is to intentional objects, joy depends both on the more objective character of things and on my subjective construal of them. If I find a desirable item on my table and construe it as a gift, I will rejoice; if I construe it as a bribe, I will become disturbed. On the one hand, joy is not entirely self-generated; because it has an object and is a response, it comes partly from outside, from the character of the world I encounter. On the other hand, I can rob myself of joy by failing to perceive good things *as* good things and to respond to them properly. I can be in a perfect world with the fruit of all trees but one available to me, but if I construe it as not good enough because the fruit of that one tree is withheld from me, I will not rejoice.

With its four structural elements (intentional object, perception of the object as good, experience of the object as unowed, and a positive hedonic response), we can define joy as *emotional attunement between the self and the world—usually a small portion of it—experienced as blessing*. To complete the sketch of joy, I need add that for the most part we don't experience joy as an all-or-nothing affair. It is neither a matter of having a perfect joy or no joy at all, nor is it a matter of joy either overriding all our emotions or of it being entirely absent. Whether joy is intense or gentle, simple or complex, episodic or enduring, joy is mostly partial and overlaps with other emotions. As the experience of joy at a funeral of one who lived life well attests, we can rejoice and grieve at the same time.

We are now about halfway into our joy lab work. By now we should be able to pick out joy from among other aspects of human life and experience. That suffices to establish that joy is an emotion much richer than happiness understood as feeling of pleasure. But to understand the connection between joy and the good life, we need to stay a bit longer in the laboratory and take a brief look at some additional and surprising features of joy.

Fleshing Out Joy

The claim that it is possible to rejoice in the midst of suffering will surprise nobody. Some people rejoice while others suffer, even because they suffer, and some people suffer so that others can rejoice (J. S. Bach of Jesus' passion: "Your bitter suffering brings thousands of joys"). Suffering and joy are here divided among different individuals. But can a person who suffers rejoice? Surprisingly, the answer is yes: we can suffer and rejoice at the same time. Of course, we don't rejoice *because* of suffering, either of our own suffering or somebody else's; such joy would be either masochistic or mean. When we rejoice while suffering it is because of some good that is ours despite the suffering (for instance, God's character, deeds, and the promise of redemption) or because of a good the suffering will produce (for instance, a child for a mother in childbirth). Put more abstractly, "joy despite" is possible on account of "joy because."

Some joys are morally neutral, but many have a positive or negative *moral* valence. Joy can be corrupt (with eyes wide open I construe an object of joy as good, but it is in fact profoundly wicked); joy can be self-absorbed (I rejoice only in my own good); joy can be indifferent to others (I rejoice with gusto over my distant friend's fortune but am unmoved by the pain at my doorstep); joy can be perverse (I rejoice in the misfortune of others); joy can be generous (I rejoice in the good of others or, to quote the New Testament, I "rejoice with those who rejoice"); joy can be attuned to the suffering of others (as when, in a period of intense joy, we continue to be mindful of those who grieve).

Since joy has a moral dimension, rejoicing can be an obligation (for instance, a command of God, as in the Hebrew Bible and in the New Testament). True, we have little control over feelings of joy; as a rule, they simply well up inside us when we perceive that some unowed good has happened to us or to those we care for. But we do have significant control over how we *construe* a situation and whether we are properly attentive to these unowed goods. The command to rejoice presupposes a belief that objectively a given situation ought rightly be construed as good. Absence of joy can then amount to an untruthful rendering of that situation. Yet, though joy can be commanded, joy cannot be imposed. A person himself or herself must engage in a construal of a situation and positive feelings must well up inside them for there to be joy. Joy is either free or it isn't joy—and that's true even of commanded joy.

Perhaps most surprisingly, joy has an activist dimension. Surprising, because joy doesn't explicitly advocate any values or social ideals; it doesn't seek to persuade others and to embody those values and ideals in social institutions. But joy wants something; all emotions do. They project themselves into the future and motivate action. What kind of future does joy want? As it projects itself into the future, joy doesn't aim directly at changing the world; it simply delights in and celebrates the good that is and proclaims, implicitly, that it is good for that good to continue to be. "All joy wants eternity—wants deep, deep eternity," wrote Friedrich Nietzsche.[3] Like love, joy is one of the "eternity-seeking" emotions. It wills itself as a permanent state. But just for that reason it also wills all the "objects" that give it rise. In this willing joy sets itself tacitly against features of the world over which one cannot or should not rejoice, and does so without resentment and judgment. As such, joy is both the beginning and the end of authentic personal, social, and political transformation.

Joy is best experienced in community. Joy seeks company ("come and rejoice with me") and the company of those who rejoice feeds

3. Friedrich Nietzsche, *Thus Spoke Zarathustra*, ed. Adrian Del Caro and Robert B. Pippin, trans. Adrian Del Caro (New York: Cambridge University Press, 2006), 264.

the joy of each. Feasts and celebrations both express and nourish joy. As feasts and celebrations illustrate, though joy is irreducibly personal—nobody can rejoice in my place!—joyfulness can also be an aura of a social space, whether a household or a larger community, so that when we enter such a space, we enter into joy, and, often, joy enters into us.

Finally, joy is not a self-standing emotion, isolated from the character and circumstances of a person rejoicing. As a form of attunement between the self and the world perceived as blessing, joy is, ultimately, the emotional dimension of the good life, of a life that is both going well and is being lived well; complete and lasting joy is the emotional side of the ultimate good.

Joy and the Good Life

With our lab work completed and the key features of joy identified, we can return to the relation between joy and the good life. In contemporary, late-modern cultures, many define the good life as a life that *feels good*, in which pleasure overshadows the pain (happiness as pleasure). Others think of the good life as life that *goes well*, a life marked either by some objective indicators of well-being or by a more subjective assessment that life is satisfying (happiness as well-being or life satisfaction). Still others, today perhaps a minority, think of the good life as the life that is *lived well*, in accordance with our nature or following divine commandments (happiness as excellent life). Advocates of these three basic ways of understanding the good life debate their positions intensely. I don't need to wade into this debate here, except to note that in my judgment, any plausible candidate for the good life has to incorporate all three: life is truly and fully good when (1) it goes well, (2) we lead it well, and (3) when it is pleasurable. Of course, to be a plausible candidate for the good life isn't yet to be a compelling one. How compelling a plausible candidate for the good life is will depend on how each of its three dimensions are construed and related to one another.

A remarkable thing about joy is that, as a single emotion, it integrates all three essential dimensions of the good life. How does it accomplish this extraordinary feat? Though in no way reducible to "pleasurable feeling," joy, one of the most pleasurable emotions, arises when a portion of our life goes well (some good has happened to us) and when we relate well to ourselves and to that portion of our lives (we perceive it as a blessing and are grateful, and, for the moment at least, content). Note that joy isn't a mere affective add-on to having led our lives well and to something good having happened to us, like a cold beer at the end of a successful hard day or a blissful spa weekend at the end of a good month. As I have noted earlier, joy isn't a self-standing emotion; it is even less a self-standing feeling. It is integrally related to (a portion of our) life going well and our life being lived well—and, as I have noted earlier, it is so even when we rejoice in the midst of suffering and in response to a command. We receive a clean bill of health (or are offered a dream job, or our marriage proposal is accepted), we experience ourselves as blessed, we feel pleasure over these things—that's joy. Of course, the doctors may have failed to detect some life-threatening illness or the job may turn out to be a nightmare or our partner may walk away a week before the wedding, and then our joy will have proven to have been false. But in all true joy, the three dimensions of the good life are integrated.

Could *joy*, then, be a candidate for a one-word definition of the good life, perhaps in the way some people think *happiness* is? Indeed, could it be better able to integrate in itself the requisite conditions for our thriving and our responsibility for it? Could the good life be described as the life of joy, as the parable of the talents might be read to suggest? Not quite. Joy is a bit like a crown. Wearing a crown won't make you into a monarch; a child can wear one, as can a usurper. If you aren't a monarch already, even if what is set on your head looks like a crown, it isn't actually a crown. For the crown is a symbol of royal authority. It is similar with joy. Joy isn't the good life; it is one part of it, the one dependent on the other two. If there isn't any good, either perceived or actual, to rejoice over—no good circumstances or active stances—happy feelings you might have may look and feel like joy, but they will not be joy. As an emotion, joy is always *over* something (perceived) as good, and it presumes proper relation to some (perceived) good—which means that *true* joy presumes proper relation to some *actual* good. At the same time, the crown is not merely external to royal authority. In a crown, royal authority comes to expression; wearing it, a monarch is publicly manifest as monarch. It is similar with joy. Joy is not merely external to the good life, a mint leaf on the cake's whipped cream. Rather, the good life expresses and manifests itself in joy. Joy is the emotional dimension of life that goes well and that is led well, a positive affective response to life going well and life being led well; all three in their interpenetrating unity—life going well, life being led well, and joy—are the good life.

For the most part, segments of our life, often entire chunks of it, aren't going well and much of it we don't live well. Given that joy attaches to life going well and being led well, must joy be lost to us? It need not be. We can rejoice over the many small goods we experience, and for those of us who are religious, we can find joy in the One Good that is both the source and the goal of our existence. Though fragmentary, all small joys celebrate goods in our lives that are and remain wonderful, at times no more than tender plants in the cracks of our otherwise heavily cemented and gray lives. And in all true joys we yearn for, and perhaps also faintly experience, a world in which all things and all manner of things shall be well.

Bibliography

Anderson, Herbert and Bonnie J. Miller-McLemore. *Faith's Wisdom for Daily Living.* Minneapolis: Augsburg Fortress, 2008.

Anderson, Herbert and Edward Foley. *Mighty Stories, Dangerous Rituals: Weaving Together the Human and the Divine.* San Francisco: Jossey-Bass, 2001.

Augustine. *Homilies on 1 John.* In *Augustine: Later Works*, edited by John Burnaby. Philadelphia: Westminster, 1955.

Balthasar, Hans Urs von. *Theo-Drama: Theological Dramatic Theory.* 5 volumes. San Francisco: Ignatius, 1988–98.

Barth, Karl. *Church Dogmatics.* 4 volumes. Edinburgh: T&T Clark, 1956–75.

Belenky, Mary Field, Lynn A. Bond, and Jacqueline S. Weinstock. *A Tradition That Has No Name: Nurturing the Development of People, Families, and Communities.* New York: Basic Books, 1999.

Benjamin, Walter. "Theses on the Philosophy of History." In *Illuminations*, edited by Hannah Arendt, translated by Harry Zohn. New York: Schocken Books, 2007.

Benz, Ernst. *Heiteres Licht der Herrlichkeit: Die Glaubenswelt der Ostkirche.* Hamburg: Furche, 1962.

Bidwell, Duane R. "Eschatology and Childhood Hope: Reflections from Work in Progress." *The Journal of Pastoral Theology* 20, no. 2 (2010).

Bidwell, Duane R. and Donald L. Batisky. "Abundance in Finitude: An Exploratory Study of Children's Accounts of Hope in Chronic Illness." *The Journal of Pastoral Theology* 19, no. 1 (2009).

Blais, André and Robert Young. "Why Do People Vote? An Experiment in Rationality." *Public Choice* 99 (1999): 39–55.

Boisen, Anton. *Out of the Depths: An Autobiographical Study of Mental Disorder and Religious Experience.* New York: Harper, 1960.

———. *Vision from a Little Known Country: A Boisen Reader.* Edited by Glenn H. Asquith. Journal of Pastoral Care Publications, 1992.

Boyle, Gregory. *Tattoos on the Heart: The Power of Boundless Compassion.* New York: Free Press, 2010.

Bruni, Luigino and Pier Luigi Porta, eds. *Economics and Happiness: Framing the Analysis.* New York: Oxford University Press, 2005.

Buechner, Frederick. *Wishful Thinking: A Theological ABC.* New York: Harper and Row, 1973.

Burnell, Peter. *The Augustinian Person.* Washington, DC: Catholic University of America Press, 2005.

Burton-Christie, Douglas. *The Word in the Desert: Scripture and the Quest for Holiness in Early Christian Monasticism.* New York: Oxford University Press, 1993.

Buytendijk, Frederik Jacobus Johannes. *Het Spel van Mensch en Diet als openbaring van levensdriften.* Amsterdam, 1932.

Byasse, Jason. *Praise Seeking Understanding.* Grand Rapids: Eerdmans, 2007.

Campbell, Colin. "I Shop Therefore I Know That I Am: The Metaphysical Foundations of Modern Consumerism." In *Elusive Consumption,* edited by Karin Ekstrom and Helen Brembeck. Oxford: Berg, 2004.

———. *The Romantic Ethic and the Spirit of Modern Consumerism.* Oxford: Basil Blackwell, 1987.

Capper, John Mark. "Karl Barth's Theology of Joy." PhD diss., University of Cambridge, 1998.

Capps, Donald. *Giving Counsel: A Minister's Guidebook.* St. Louis: Chalice, 2001.

Carr, Alan. *Positive Psychology: The Science of Happiness and Human Strengths.* 2nd ed. New York: Routledge, 2011.

Casanova, José. *Public Religions in the Modern World.* Chicago: The University of Chicago Press, 1994.

Charry, Ellen. *God and the Art of Happiness.* Grand Rapids: Eerdmans, 2010.

———. "The Necessity of Divine Happiness: A Response from Systematic Theology." In *The Bible and the Pursuit of Happiness: What the Old and the New Testaments Teach Us about the Good Life,* edited by Brent A. Strawn. New York: Oxford University Press, 2012.

Clarke, Bill. *Enough Room for Joy: The Early Days of Jean Vanier's L'Arche.* New York: BlueBridge, 2007.

Clebsch, William A. and Charles R. Jaekle, eds. *Pastoral Care in Historical Perspective.* New York: Jason Aronson, 1994.

Clinebell, Howard J., Jr. *Contemporary Growth Therapies.* Nashville: Abingdon, 1983.

Cole, Allan Hugh, Jr. *Be Not Anxious: Pastoral Care of Disquieted Souls.* Grand Rapids: Eerdmans, 2008.

Cone, James H. *The Spirituals and the Blues: An Interpretation.* New York: Seabury, 1972.

Cooey, Paula M. *Religious Imagination and the Body: A Feminist Analysis.* New York: Oxford University Press, 1994.

———. *Willing the Good: Jesus, Dissent, and Desire.* Minneapolis: Augsburg Fortress, 2006.

Cooke, Alistair, ed. *The Vintage Mencken.* New York: Vintage Books, 1955.

Csikszentmihalyi, Mihaly. *Flow: The Psychology of Optimal Experience.* New York: Harper Perennial, 2008.

Daloz, Laurent A. Parks, Cheryl H. Keen, James P. Keen, and Sharon Daloz Parks. *Common Fire: Leading Lives of Commitment in a Complex World.* Boston: Beacon, 1996.

DeMarinis, Valery M. *Critical Caring: A Feminist Model for Pastoral Psychology.* Louisville: Westminster John Knox, 1994.

Dillard, Annie. *The Writing Life.* New York: Harper and Row, 1989.

Dodaro, Robert. *Christ and the Just Society in the Thought of Augustine.* New York: Cambridge University Press, 2004.

Doehring, Carrie. *The Practice of Pastoral Care: A Postmodern Approach.* Louisville: Westminster John Knox, 2006.

Dostoyevsky, Fyodor. *The Brothers Karamazov.* Translated by Constance Garnett. New York: The Modern Library, 1929.

Farmer, Paul. *Partner to the Poor: A Paul Farmer Reader.* Edited by Haun Saussy. Berkeley: University of California Press, 2010.

Ford, David F. and Daniel W. Hardy. *Living in Praise: Worshipping and Knowing God.* Rev. ed. Grand Rapids: Baker, 2005.

Francis (pope). *The Joy of the Gospel: Apostolic Exhortation Evangelii Gaudium of the Holy Father Francis to the Bishops, Clergy, Consecrated Persons and the Lay Faithful on the Proclamation of the Gospel in Today's World.* 2013.

Frank, Robert H., Thomas Gilovich, and Dennis T. Regan. "Do Economists Make Bad Citizens?" *Journal of Economic Perspectives* 10, no. 1 (Winter 1996): 187–92.

———. "Does Studying Economics Inhibit Cooperation?" *Journal of Economic Perspectives* 7, no. 2 (Spring 1993): 159–71.

Frederick, Marla. "Rags to Riches: Religion, Media, and the Performance of Wealth in a Neoliberal Age." In *Ethnographies of Neoliberalism*, edited by Carol Greenhouse. Philadelphia: University of Pennsylvania Press, 2009.

Freud, Sigmund. *Studies in Hysteria.* Translated and edited by James Strachey. New York: Basic Books, 1957.

Frey, Bruno S. and Stephan Meier. "Are Political Economists Selfish and Indoctrinated? Evidence from a Natural Experiment." *Economic Inquiry* 41, no. 3 (July 2003): 448–62.

Fuller, Robert C. *Wonder: From Emotion to Spirituality.* Chapel Hill: University of North Carolina Press, 2006.

Gay, Volney P. *Joy and the Objects of Psychoanalysis: Literature, Belief, and Neurosis.* New York: State University of New York Press, 2001.

Goldingay, John. *Psalms 1–41.* Baker Commentary on the Old Testament Wisdom and Psalms, vol. 1. Grand Rapids: Baker, 2006.

Graham, Carol. *The Pursuit of Happiness: An Economy of Well-Being.* Washington, DC: Brookings Institution Press, 2011.

Graham, Larry Kent. *Care of Persons, Care of Worlds: A Psychosystems Approach.* Nashville: Abingdon, 1992.

Harrison, Carol. *Augustine: Christian Truth and Fractured Humanity.* New York: Oxford University Press, 2000.

Holifield, Brooks. *A History of Pastoral Care in America.* Nashville: Abingdon, 1983.

Holmes, Barbara A. *Joy Unspeakable: Contemplative Practices in the Black Church.* Minneapolis: Fortress Press, 2004.

Isaac, Jeffery. "Critics of Totalitarianism." In *The Cambridge History of Twentieth-Century Political Thought,* edited by Terrence Ball and Richard Bellamy. New York: Cambridge University Press, 2003.

James, William. "The Moral Equivalent of War." In *Writings: 1902–1910.* New York: Library of America, 1987.

———. "On a Certain Blindness in Human Beings." In *On Some of Life's Ideals.* New York: Henry Holt and Co., 1912.

———. *Talks to Teachers on Psychology.* Cambridge, MA: Harvard University Press, 1983.

———. *The Varieties of Religious Experience: A Study in Human Nature.* Edited by Martin Marty. Hammondsworth: Penguin, 1982.

Jennings, Willie. "Joy That Gathers." Yale Center for Faith and Culture, August 21, 2014. http://faith.yale.edu/sites/default/files/jennings_-_joy_that_gathers.pdf.

Justes, Emma J. *Hearing beyond the Words: How to Become a Listening Pastor.* Nashville: Abingdon, 2006.

Kidder, Tracy. *Mountains beyond Mountains.* New York: Random House, 2004.

Kleiber, Douglas, Gordon Walker, and Roger Mannell. *A Social Psychology of Leisure.* State College, PA: Venture Books, 2011.

Kujawa-Holbrook, Sheryl A. and Karen B. Montagno, eds. *Injustice and the Care of Souls.* Minneapolis: Fortress Press, 2009.

Lane, Robert. *The Loss of Happiness in Market Democracies.* New Haven: Yale University Press, 2001.

———. *The Market Experience.* New York: Cambridge University Press, 1991.

Lear, Jonathan. *Happiness, Death, and the Remainder of Life.* Cambridge, MA: Harvard University Press, 2002.

Lewis, C. S. *Surprised by Joy: The Shape of My Early Life.* New York: Harcourt Brace, 1955.

MacIntyre, Alasdair. *After Virtue.* 2nd ed. Notre Dame: University of Notre Dame Press, 1984.

Marion, Jean-Luc. *The Erotic Phenomenon.* Translated by Stephen E. Lewis. Chicago: The University of Chicago Press, 2006.

Marx, Karl. "Contribution to the Critique of Hegel's *Philosophy of Right*." In *The Marx-Engels Reader*, edited by Robert C. Tucker. 2nd ed. New York: W. W. Norton & Company, 1978.

Maslow, Abraham. *Religions, Values, and Peak-Experiences.* New York: Penguin, 1994.

McMahan, Ethan A. and David Estes. "Hedonic versus Eudaimonic Conceptions of Well-Being: Evidence of Differential Associations with Self-reported Well-Being." *Social Indicators Research* 103 (2011): 93–108.

McMahon, Darrin M. *Happiness: A History*. New York: Atlantic Monthly, 2006.

Miller-McLemore, Bonnie J. *In the Midst of Chaos: Caring for Children as Spiritual Practice*. San Francisco: Jossey-Bass, 2007.

———. "The Living Human Web: Pastoral Theology at the Turn of the Century," In *Through the Eyes of Women*, edited by Jeanne Stevenson-Moessner. Minneapolis: Fortress Press, 1996.

———. "The Subversive Practice of Christian Theology." In *Christian Theology in Practice*, ed. Bonnie J. Miller-McLemore. Grand Rapids: Eerdmans, 2011.

Moltmann, Jürgen. *Ethics of Hope*. Translated by Margaret Kohl. Minneapolis: Fortress Press, 2012.

———. *Sun of Righteousness, Arise! God's Future for Humanity and the Earth*. Minneapolis: Fortress Press, 2010.

———. *Theology and Joy*. London: SCM, 1973.

———. *Theology of Play*. New York: Harper & Row, 1972.

Morrice, William. *Joy in the New Testament*. Grand Rapids: Eerdmans, 1984.

Moschella, Mary Clark. "Positive Psychology as a Resource for Pastoral Theology and Care: A Preliminary Assessment." *The Journal of Pastoral Theology* 21, no. 1 (2011).

Murdoch, Iris. "Metaphysics and Ethics." In *The Nature of Metaphysics*, edited by D. F. Pears. London: MacMillan, 1960.

Neuger, Christie Cozad. "Narrative Therapy." In *The Concise Dictionary of Pastoral Care and Counseling*, edited by Glenn H. Asquith Jr. Nashville: Abingdon, 2010.

Neumark, Heidi B. *Breathing Space: A Spiritual Journey in the South Bronx*. Boston: Beacon, 2003.

Nietzsche, Friedrich. *Thus Spoke Zarathustra*. Edited by Adrian Del Caro and Robert B. Pippin. Translated by Adrian Del Caro. New York: Cambridge University Press, 2006.

Nouwen, Henri. *Adam: God's Beloved*. Maryknoll: Orbis, 1997.

———. *Bread for the Journey: A Daybook of Wisdom and Faith*. San Francisco: HarperSanFrancisco, 1997.

Parks, Sharon Daloz. *Big Questions, Worthy Dreams: Mentoring Emerging Adults in Their Search for Meaning, Purpose, and Faith*. Rev. ed. San Francisco: Jossey-Bass, 2011.

Pascal, Blaise. *Pensées sur la religion et sur quelques autres sujets*. Edited by Louis Lafuma. Paris: Editions de Luxembourg, 1951.

———. *Pensées*. Translated by A. J. Krailsheimer. Baltimore: Penguin Books, 1966.

Pecchi, Lorenzo. *Revisiting Keynes: Economic Possibilities for Our Grandchildren*. Cambridge, MA: MIT Press, 2010.

Petrović, Đorđe. PhD diss., Pontificium Institutum Orientale. 2015.

Pippin, Robert. "Nietzsche on Naïve and Clumsy Lovers." In *Idealism as Modernism: Hegelian Variations*. New York: Cambridge University Press, 1997.

Plessner, Helmuth. *Lachen und Weinen*. Bern: Francke, 1961.

Portmann, Adolf. *Biologie und Geist*. Freiburg: Herder, 1963.

Rahner, Hugo. *Man at Play*. New York: Herder & Herder, 1967.

Ramsay, Nancy. *Pastoral Care and Counseling: Redefining the Paradigms*. Nashville: Abingdon, 2004.

Robinson, John P. "Sex, Arts, and Verbal Abilities: Three Further Indicators of How American Life Is Not Improving." *Social Indicators Research* 99 (2010): 1–12.

Santner, Eric. *On the Psychotheology of Everyday Life: Reflections on Freud and Rosenzweig*. Chicago: The University of Chicago Press, 2001.

Savage, John. *Listening and Caring Skills in Ministry: A Guide for Groups and Leaders*. Nashville: Abingdon, 1995.

Scalise, Charles J. *Bridging the Gap*. Nashville: Abingdon, 2003.

Schiller, Friedrich. "An die Freude/Ode to Joy." Translated by William F. Wertz. Schiller Institute. http://www.schillerinstitute.org/transl/schiller_poem/ode_to_joy.pdf.

Schmemann, Alexander. *The Journals of Father Alexander Schmemann 1973–1983.* Translated by Juliana Schmemann. Crestwood: St. Vladimir's Seminary Press, 2000.

Schniewind, Julius. *Die Freude der Buße.* Göttingen: Vandenhoeck & Ruprecht, 1956.

Scitovsky, Tibor. *The Joyless Economy: The Psychology of Human Satisfaction.* Rev. ed. New York: Oxford University Press, 1992.

Shoop, Marcia Mount. *Let the Bones Dance: Embodiment and the Body of Christ.* Louisville: Westminster John Knox, 2010.

Son, Angella. "Agents of Joy: A New Image of Pastoral Care." *The Journal of Pastoral Theology* 18, no.1 (2008).

Steiner, George. *Tolstoy or Dostoevsky: An Essay in the Old Criticism.* 2nd ed. New Haven: Yale University Press, 1996.

Stevenson, Robert Louis. *The Lantern-Bearers and Other Essays.* Edited by Jeremy Traglown. New York: First Cooper Square, 1999.

Stokes, Allison. *Ministry after Freud.* New York: Pilgrim, 1985.

Stout, Jeffrey. *Democracy and Tradition.* Princeton: Princeton University Press, 2004.

Strawn, Brent A., ed. *The Bible and the Pursuit of Happiness: What the Old and New Testaments Teach Us about the Good Life.* Oxford: Oxford University Press, 2012.

Sundermeier, Theo. *Religion—was ist das? Religionswissenschaft im theologischen Kontext.* Frankfurt: O. Lembeck, 2007.

Sunstein, Cass and Richard Thaler. *Nudge: Improving Decisions about Health, Wealth, and Happiness.* New York: Penguin Books, 2009.

Tillich, Paul. *The Courage to Be.* New Haven: Yale University Press, 1952.

Tomasi, John. *Liberalism beyond Justice: Citizens, Society and the Boundaries of Political Theory*. Princeton: Princeton University Press, 2001.

Troeger, Thomas. *Wonder Reborn: Creating Sermons on Hymns, Music, and Poetry*. New York: Oxford University Press, 2010.

Tutu, Desmond and Mpho A. Tutu. *Made for Goodness: And Why This Makes All the Difference*. New York: HarperOne, 2010.

Voscamp, Ann. *One Thousand Gifts: A Dare to Live Fully Right Where You Are*. Grand Rapids: Zondervan, 2010.

Way, Peggy. *Created by God: Pastoral Care for All God's Creatures*. St. Louis: Chalice, 2005.

Wise, Carroll. *The Meaning of Pastoral Care*. New York: Harper and Row, 1966.

Acknowledgments

This collection grew out of a consultation held in September 2012 on joy and human flourishing at the Yale Center for Faith and Culture, for which Charles Mathewes, Jürgen Moltmann, Mary Clark Moschella, and Marianne Meye Thompson first prepared the essays included here. It was made possible by the astounding and abiding generosity of Alonzo McDonald and the McDonald Agape Foundation. Unique among donors, Al attended the consultation itself and was a full participant in our conversations; thanks are due first to him, not only for his financial support of the project but also for the insights he shared with us. Thanks, too, are due Christopher Corbin—now a doctoral student at Vanderbilt University—who spearheaded much of the consultation's organization before Justin began work at the Center, as well as Jan O'Dell, who was the Center's administrative assistant at the time. Jennifer Herdt and John Hare, coinvestigators with Miroslav on the Center's God and Human Flourishing project, contributed substantially to the consultation itself and have been invaluable partners in conceiving this project's future lines of inquiry. Charles Coury (then a member of the Center's board) also gave generously of his time and understanding in participating in our conversations.

147

Since the first gathering in 2012, the Center has undertaken a series of consultations on the "Theology of Joy" as a part of a planning grant provided by the John Templeton Foundation, for whose support of the Center's continuing vocation and work we are very grateful. This volume's essays by N. T. Wright and Miroslav were written for those consultations, which were ably organized and executed by the Center's Director of Research and Publication, Matthew Croasmun—dialogue partner par excellence and a good friend—and administrative assistant, Allison Van Rhee. Others at the Center for Faith and Culture have provided much support in the editing of this volume. We are thankful especially to our managing director, Skip Masback, for his unflagging support of our work and encouragement of our vocations, and fellow researcher and friend Ryan McAnnally-Linz. Charles Gillespie and Jewelle Bickel are also to be thanked for providing valuable feedback on the shape of the introduction. Finally, we are grateful to our editor at Fortress Press, Michael Gibson, for believing in the potential of this project, for stewarding it to completion, and for his abundant patience with us as we pursued it.

To pursue such work, on matters of great human moment and the substance of what makes life worth living, is a blessing over which we abound in rejoicing. It is in that spirit that we offer this collection to you.

Miroslav Volf and *Justin E. Crisp*

Contributors

Justin E. Crisp, doctoral student in theology at Yale University and doctoral fellow of the Yale Center for Faith and Culture.

Charles Mathewes, Carolyn M. Barbour Professor of Religious Studies at the University of Virginia.

Jürgen Moltmann, professor emeritus of systematic theology at the University of Tübingen.

Mary Clark Moschella, Roger J. Squire Professor of Pastoral Care and Counseling at Yale Divinity School.

Marianne Meye Thompson, George Eldon Ladd Professor of New Testament at Fuller Theological Seminary.

Miroslav Volf, Henry B. Wright Professor of Systematic Theology at Yale Divinity School and Founding Director of the Yale Center for Faith and Culture.

N.T. Wright, Professor of New Testament and Early Christianity at the University of St. Andrews.

Index